The Country in the Mirror

Poems of Protest and Witness

Edited by

Sharon Darrow

Rootstock Publishing

Montpelier, VT

The Country in the Mirror
©2026 Sharon Darrow

Release Date: April 21, 2026

All Rights Reserved.
Printed in the USA.

Paperback ISBN: 978-1-57869-221-7

Library of Congress Control Number: 2026934239

Published by Rootstock Publishing
an imprint of Ziggy Media, LLC
Montpelier, VT 05602

info@rootstockpublishing.com
www.rootstockpublishing.com

Cover art "The Weary World," cut paper by ©Martha Elmes.

Book and cover design by Eddie Vincent, ENC Graphic Services.

Previously published poems are reprinted by permission of the author
(see Credits page).

For reprint permissions or to schedule a poetry reading, contact Sharon Darrow
at SharonDarrow@hotmail.com.

Dedicated to our children and grandchildren.
And to the poets and resisters who bear witness.

In memoriam:

Baron Wormser
Renée Nicole Good

Contents

Introduction   1

Winter: Prophecy Against Those

No Earth and No Heaven / *Paul Hoover*   7

A soul nosedives into a body doomed. Angel bound. / *cin salach*   8

On the Day of the Election, I Think of the Video of My Nephew's First Mountain Bike Ride with His Father, a Long Haul Covid Survivor / *Sean Prentiss*   9

Prophecy Against Those / *Chard deNiord*   12

Believe Them / *Erika Nichols-Frazer*   14

Jon Batiste's Piano, Super Bowl 2025 / *Sharon Darrow*   15

I-89 from Vermont to Canada in Winter / *Tricia Knoll*   16

Neighbor / *Judith Janoo*   17

The Green of Greenland / *David M. Katz*   19

Complicity / *Alexander Anlyan*   21

Today's Horrorscope / *John Foy*   22

I woke up thinking of them / *Arlene Iris Distler*   24

I Choke on Grace / *Nikki Grimes*   26

Candle / *Christine DePetrillo*   27

Border Fugue / *Amit Majmudar*   28

The Snake / *Martín Espada*   29

Aunt Esther / *Stephen Bluestone*   30

Seed Shock / *Eva Zimet*   31

Subtext / *Aria Dominguez*   32

Shouldering / *Rachel Hadas*   33

Child at the Wheel / *Wyatt Townley*   34

Baby Hitler / *Louise Hawes*   35

The Ministry of Frost / *Meredith Bergmann*   36

Loss of Intrigue / *Scott Withiam*   37

Rain or Shine / *James Bird*   38

Americans in Love / *Mike Puican*   39

Hotel Mar-a-lago / *Thomas Schmidt*   40

Spring: The Way Things Were Up Until Now

Signs and Wonders / *Paul Hoover*   45
The Way Things Were Up Until Now / *Bianca Stone*   48
Sunday Morning Haiku / *Mike Puican*   50
"Ask What" / *Meredith Bergmann*   51
What We're Not Supposed to Say / *Pamela Ahlen*   52
What Am I Waiting For? / *Sharon Darrow*   53
Blues / *Sydney Lea*   55
"Here pity only lives when it is dead" / *Henry Weinfield*   56
All That Life / *Elisabeth Fred*   59
Passover Poem of Pain—Gaza / *Arlene Iris Distler*   60
Get Here / *Amy Allen*   61
The Still Small Possibility / *Judith Janoo*   62
Abject Cruelty / *Sandy Edmonds*   63
Tanatofobia: Fear of Losing Your Mexican Mother / *Rigoberto González*   64
The Iguanas Skitter Through the Cemetery by the Sea / *Martín Espada*   65
Corrido del ciclista / *Raúl Dorantes*   67
Corrido of the Cyclist / *Raúl Dorantes (translated by Mary Hawley)*   69
Questionnaire / *Alison McGhee*   71
Hunger / *Mary Meriam*   72
To the Tune of "Veni redemptor gentium" by Ambrose of Milan / *Jee Leong Koh*   73
Stand by and Listen for the Whistle / *JPayne*   75
That Gritty, Bright, Shadowless Sunlight / *Ron Lay-Sleeper*   76
Today, I Figured I Should Finally Get Rid / *Kauakanilehua Māhoe Adams*   77
The Truth as Well / *Rachel Hadas*   79
Pandemonium / *Tim Wynne-Jones*   83

Summer: You Think This Is Hot?

As a Lion in Secret Places / *Paul Hoover*   87
Naming Light / *Mike Puican*   89

Don't Worry / *Cindy Faughnan*   90

Florida's Famous For: / *Beth Kanell*   91

It disturbs me / *Joyce Thomas*   92

Wrecking Ball & the muskrats / *daithí*   94

Take to the Streets, February 15, 2003 / *Judith Janoo*   95

No Kings / *Sharon Darrow*   96

On the way to the protest / *Joanne M. Giannino*   97

Rising / *Louella Bryant*   99

Fierce Compassion / *Amabel Kylee Siorghlas*   100

Frog / *Lynn Ungar*   102

Fire and Flood and Bureau Drawer / *Rachel Hadas*   103

The Perfect Space / *Madeleine May Kunin*   105

Shoelaces / *Steve Minkin*   106

Rhapsody on a Line by Poe / *Amit Majmudar*   107

Contradiction / *Mary Cheyne*   108

Jus Soli / *Nancy Stewart*   109

In Thinking / *Chard deNiord*   110

The Pigeon Parade / *S. J. Cahill*   111

My Broken Mirror / *James Bird*   112

I have never loved America more / *Julie Berry*   113

The Inheritance / *Gregory Maguire*   114

The Bataan Death March / *Terry Hauptman*   115

This Goes On and On / *John Steffler*   117

The Guadalupe Camp Mystic July 2025 / *Kathi Appelt*   119

You Think This is Hot? / *Garret Keizer*   121

Raven's Protest Poem (from the film Unseen) / *Shalom Gorewitz*   122

How to Offer Hope / *cin salach*   123

Aftermath Posturing / *Scott Withiam*   126

I Am the Very Model of a Narcissistic Slanderer /
    Tim Wynne-Jones   128

Fall: It's the Beginning of the End...

The Dry Bones / *Paul Hoover*   131

Palimpsest / *Katherine Quimby*   133

Labor Day / *Elisabeth Fred*   134

The Candidates Debate / *Mike Puican*   135

Election / *Wyatt Townley*   136

It's the Beginning of the End and I'm Here to Tell You /
   Samantha Kolber   137

The Right Tyrant / *Julie Larios*   139

Trump, a Philippic / *Chard deNiord*   141

american dog / *Chris Solís Green*   142

The Edge of the Gorge / *Judith Janoo*   143

The Watchlist / *Alyx Young*   145

White House Peace Vigil / *Robin Galbraith*   147

The climb / *Katie Moritz*   153

The Elephant in the Room / *Amanda West Lewis*   154

What the Alt National Park Service Taught Me / *Susen James*   156

Destination Despair / *S. J. Cahill*   157

Final Exam / *Scott Withiam*   158

Have You Ever Met a Nefarian? / *Shalom Gorewitz*   161

October 2025 / *Jennifer Franklin*   162

Homenaje a los silbatos / *Raúl Dorantes*   163

Homage to the Whistles / *Raúl Dorantes*
   (translated by Mary Hawley)   165

First Tipping Point, October 13, 2025 / *Sharon Darrow*   167

Forest / *Mary Meriam*   169

Mud Covenant / *Mary Meriam*   170

Colossus / *Mary Meriam*   171

I Mostly Ignore the Horrors / *Adrienne Gruber*   172

A Delicate Balance / *Louise Hawes*   173

Riding on a Cloud / *Rachel Hadas*   174

The day a poet is murdered by ICE / *Hannah Eve Levy*   176

I Long to See Her Unharmed Breathing Air the Earth Is Meant
   to Breathe / *Nathalie Canessa Kramer*   177

¡SÍ, SE PUEDE! / *Simki Ghebremichael*   180

grace like time is everywhere / *Sarah B Sullivan*   182

Besiege Your Siege / *Terry Hauptman*   183

Mary / *John Foy*   185

The Country in the Mirror / *Wyatt Townley*   186

Four Years / *Doug Anderson*   193

Dare / *Christine DePetrillo* ... 195

The Survivors' Revolution / *Sharon Darrow* ... 197

Well Being / *Judith Janoo* ... 199

Poets / *Pete Blose* ... 200

Poetic Justice / *Amanda Harris* ... 201

Symphony in Hope Major / *Kelly Bennett* ... 203

The World up Close / *cin salach* ... 204

The Allegory of Elms / *Tim Mayo* ... 205

A Gathering / *Jim Schley* ... 206

N'envoyez pas de fleurs / *Jean-Blaise Bourque* ... 208

Do Not Send Flowers / translation by *Jean-Blaise Bourque* ... 210

Cut Flowers / *Susan Gillis* ... 212

Mourning Dove / *Bill Pendergraft* ... 213

All of Us, Singing / *Liz Garton Scanlon* ... 214

Acknowledgments ... 216

Credits ... 216

Contributors Bios ... 218

Index of Contributors ... 228

Introduction

In March 2025, feeling frustrated and overwhelmed by the political and governmental changes being wrought in the United States of America, my country, I realized the only thing that felt a little like a response to me was writing poetry. In a gathering of people who were also confused and motivated to respond, I realized that other poets might feel the same way, which led me to offer a workshop in the poetry and song of protest and witness. I used *Against Forgetting: Twentieth Century Poetry of Witness*, edited by Carolyn Forché, as a take-off point. Each session we reread this poem, the book's epigraph:

Motto

In the dark times, will there also be singing?
Yes, there will be singing.
About the dark times.
—Bertolt Brecht

In the last workshop session, during a conversation about how to go forward, we decided writing the poems wasn't enough; we needed to share them. One of the members, Anne, and I planned to find a way to do that. This anthology is the result of that decision.

We wanted the book to be a place for many voices to come together and be comfortable with one another. This resulted in an eclectic mix of styles and perspectives and opinions. Some of the poets have been writing poetry for years; some are famous, others are beginners, and some are offering their first poems here as their first published works. To me—a poet who loves playing with forms and enjoys reading all sorts of approaches to poetry for adults and for young people—this feels, well, just great. Also, as a teacher of writing for many years, I love seeing new writers arrive on the scene and I admire how the veterans welcome those new voices. In this volume, despite all our ostensible differences, we have the same goal, which makes for a kind of unity in diversity, a fine goal in itself.

Some of us are poets who write for children and young adults, as well as adults. I believe we write for and read poems to children because, as Friedrich Nietzsche said, "We have art so that we shall not die of reality." We have a responsibility to find a way not to allow reality to overwhelm us as adults, and young people need the same. We cannot let them or ourselves be overcome by the reality of dark times.

Some of us are Vermonters who have been cruelly forced to deal with the reality of climate change these last few years. In the summers of 2023, 2024, and 2025 on July 10 and 11, many parts of the state have been devastated by recurring floods. It hit home for me and my neighbors living along a brook in the Northeast Kingdom of Vermont when, in two of those years, the flooding severely damaged and closed a nearby bridge. That old bridge has huge pocked concrete railings embossed with the date 1928 on an end pedestal. That was the year Vermont had to rebuild after the terrible Flood of 1927. Unlike 2025, that year we had a United States president who made sure federal help came to little Vermont. This year, the current president refused to send help of any kind, a distressing, depressing situation, especially for those who lost their homes or livelihoods. However, as Vermonters we can all take heart from what taciturn President Calvin "Silent Cal" Coolidge said at Bennington on September 21, 1928 on that long-ago occasion:

> "If the spirit of liberty should vanish in other parts of the
> union and support of our institutions should languish,
> it could all be replenished from the generous store held
> by the people of this brave little state of Vermont."

Many of the poets in this anthology are Vermonters. Some were born here, others simply lucky enough to have found a home here. I am not a native Vermonter, but I have come to understand the "spirit of liberty" that still permeates these Green Mountains and that resides deep within the people who love them. I know that spirit shall not vanish from the hearts of "the people of this brave little state of Vermont."

As a Vermonter and an American, I am determined to continue to exercise my freedom of expression and I am honored to have other voices join me as we remind each other of the liberties we have as Americans, especially as we enter 2026, the United States of America's 250th year, and caution of the potential for their loss. In March, I wondered why nothing was being done about what was happening in our country and then I realized maybe the response has to come from us—all of us. But it has to start somewhere, somewhere small and modest, but somewhere that insists on being free. Maybe it has to start here, with me, with *us*.

What follows are many poets' voices, not all of those who might have joined us, or who might still join us in their own places and in their own ways, but it's a start.

—*Sharon Darrow*
January 2026

Winter: Prophecy Against Those

No Earth and No Heaven

In the second year of the forty-fifth king,
in a time of deprivation, wars that never end,
and the death of the senses,
an average man, a prophet,
appeared in the land.
But for him there was no past;
he could not declare the future,
and the present was here to stay.
His heaven was upholstered;
the earth had disappeared.
His swimming pool's blue water
was scented with chlorine.
As he cleaned it with a net—
one leaf, two, were removed,
but the burden was not lifted.
How mottled they were in his hand,
how average the night to come.
His wife slept with her back turned,
and he responded with his.

(Haggai)

Paul Hoover

A soul nosedives into a body doomed. Angel bound.

No fair no fair no fair, dark skin, white air

We sing circles around our fear and our fear begins to spin and

Church bells answer

God nods.

Nowhere before has this never happened this way.

We whisper this into the ear of someone we know so we know the
        hearing is heard.

cin salach

On the Day of the Election, I Think of the Video of My Nephew's First Mountain Bike Ride with His Father, a Long Haul Covid Survivor

For J.

1.

In the video, R., only four, slithers down Hartman Rock's
single track, arcing into each turn as his tires whirl across
coarse dirt, spitting sandstone, passing prickly pear cactus.

Speeding, R. shouts at his father, *Is this the real world?*

   2.

I know, while watching
     the video, that R. is talking about
         the speed, the single track,
            the thrill,
       but, today, on the day of
   the election, I wonder if R.
            is also talking about
            biking with his father,
     something he hasn't
been able to do
    as his father,
    my brother, nearly
       died
        time
          and again,
            from covid,
       is still
         just a ghost,
      a wisp,
     of himself.

3.

This video is of one of the few rides J. has taken these past eight
months, too sick to do much more than just shuffle.

In the video, which I watch again and again, as four-year-old
R. banks into a turn, he bellows,

Is this the real world?

4.

I replay the video—*Is this the real world?*—tears running down my face,
my brother eight months covid sick, no end, no end, and a president
up for reelection who tells us doctors lie, masks are useless, science
is false.

5.

Is this the real world?

Is this the real world?

Is this the real world?

Is this the real world?   *Is this the real world?*
    Is this the real world?

6.

No, R., your day in Hartman's was not
just a dream, your father today
not still too sick
to mountain bike with you again,
your president—hopefully
voted out today

—claiming covid
is easier than
the flu.

Is this the real world?

    7.

Today, at this moment, let us vote with pens and voices, love and fury,
postage stamps and muscles to protect children like R. and people
like his father, who aren't even statistics.

Is this the real world?

- 231,000 covid deaths,
                preventable.
- 9.38 million covid cases,
                rising 93,581 a day.
- And untallied—
                like disenfranchised votes—
                so many covid long haul
                patients, including J.
- And untallied—
                like a rejected ballot—
                the number of children
                of long haul parents, including R.

    8.

Today, R., let us create the world anew.

Climb upon your bike and ride, forever shouting,

                Is this the real world?

                Sean Prentiss

Prophecy Against Those

They will grow ass's ears and stand
and stand like guards at the funerals of their own mothers.

They will forget history as if it were
a bad memory they can live without.

They will become victims of their own crimes.

They will confuse art with propaganda and advertisements.

They will be devoid of human leaps and other lives.

They will become famous for their towers.

They will pass eye exams year after year.

They will grow blind to others.

They will cease from studying tragedy
and find humor in violence.

They will dress sharply and abuse women.

They will deny their loneliness on the street
and hone their wit.

They will get ahead.

They will have no literature.

They will turn into boards with infinite splinters.

They will misprize and misprize.

They will see no connection between themselves
and a hazelnut.

They will destroy the Earth with luxuries.

They will recoil with disdain at poetry.

They will take pride in their faithlessness
and win at the table.

They will do what they want
and laugh at Orpheus.

They will sew lids to their lids
and carry knives to school.

They will lose the mouth to their soul's great hunger.

They will dream unceasingly of cocks crowing.

Chard deNiord

Believe Them

"When people show you who they are, believe them."
—Maya Angelou

They said they would come for us and they came.
Not with pitchforks but with flags.
They shouted *peace* while attacking a sanctuary,
freedom while controlling our bodies.

What they said they would do they did with fervor,
with violence, with a smile. We saw this coming.

Everything will be fine, they said but what they meant was,
I will be fine.
I am safe.

Erika Nichols-Frazer

Jon Batiste's Piano, Super Bowl 2025

Early February, caught between solstice and equinox,
between aging democracy and budding oligarchy,
between where we once belonged and where
unelected corrupt wealth is taking us.
Jon Batiste sang the "Star-Spangled Banner,"
accompanying himself on his joyful piano,
painted by his wife during thirty-six good hours
between chemotherapy treatments, cancer
at bay for a few joy-filled moments, pastel
swirls like butterfly wings across the light.
Weeping, I wondered at where we are now,
caught between the promise of health,
tax money used for necessary cancer research,
or that money falling into deep secret pockets.
Where will we find ourselves among the free?
Will we still belong to the band of the brave?

Sharon Darrow

I-89 from Vermont to Canada in Winter

The Canadian border is less than an hour north.
Our countries have history. Good neighbors,
borrow and offer. Fight side by side.
I get my power through Hydro-Quebec.
Canadians come to shop, ski, hike
icefish, and mountain bike. I drive north
for museums and botanical gardens. Maple sap
runs both ways. Sugar shacks boil
here and there. I love the maple leaf flag
as much as the blue and yellow of Ukraine.
We share shock and a blood moon.
So close now

to winter's big thaw. My eyes downcast.
As if every winter pothole
might eat me, vomit me out.
Black slush banks the highway,
a salt road gleams white.
Once fleeing to Canada seemed
like an escape-hatch. Love
your neighbor. Don't beggar them.
Will Canadians forgive?
The border is less than an hour away.
We are so very close.

Tricia Knoll

Neighbor

I have borrowed notes
from the organ of the night.
I have played them
on our border where
I've waited for your lavender
to gush into blossom, your fields
to scent miles of quiet.

I have walked between
your ice sculptures in this *winter
of discontent.* Each glazed figure,
animal, diplomat, village,
a window to friendship,
seeing in, seeing through.

I have taken in smoke
of burning forests, yours
and mine, and static meant
to bank on fear, churn us,
separate us, break down
power lines. Yet in nearness,
our voices can pass through
cans and string I'll keep tuning
until the static is gone.

I have measured harmony
in lavender chords,
my thoughts ruffled
by the raised feathers
of gray jay and eagle,
who will still be neighbors
when we wake tomorrow.

I will hold a note until
you come in,
until stars go cold,
I'll watch for your geese
to nest again in my pond.

Judith Janoo

The Green of Greenland

"And we rebuild our cities, not dream of islands."
    —W.H. Auden, from "Paysage Moralisé"

Rare earth was what the tyrant sought to gain,
His price of peace for Greenland and Ukraine.
Rather than green paper bills, or coin,
He would remit a currency of air,
Helium to Ukraine and Greenland
For frigid tundra and embattled souls.

He would pay no interest on the price of souls.
He knew they wouldn't yield sufficient gain.
Yet he nattered on about the wealth of Greenland,
Saw in its ice the same grift as Ukraine.
He dreamed in Florida of Arctic air
Redeemed for tankers teeming with Bitcoin.

He dreamed his face was on a silver coin,
The chief and chairman of eight billion souls.
By day he spawned an atmosphere of air
Hot as the planet that he sought to gain
Starting with the surrender of Ukraine
And the deep-mined plunder of Greenland.

The biggest island in the world, Greenland
Could lure a king in search of boundless coin
And conquest. But a modest town in Ukraine
Would be harder to obtain than all the souls
Of Greenland, so the tyrant sought first gain
From Denmark's island, despite its colder air.

He pretzel-twisted words, spewed forth an air
Of constant twaddle, such as this: Greenland
Is the most strategic land to gain

To protect us from catastrophe, the coin
Of the realm in national defense. But our souls
Cried out: Rebuild the cities of Ukraine,

Forget the pelf of Greenland and Ukraine,
And keep your hands off Panama! Your air,
The air of filthy lucre, carries souls
To hell. Erik the Red sailed west to Greenland,
Gave it that lovely name to lure the coin
Of settlement and exiles out for gain.

Souls continue hovering in Ukraine.
The gain the tyrant grabs melts into air.
The green of Greenland can't be bought for coin.

David M. Katz

Complicity

It's a small town, we have Community suppers, had one tonight,
sharing the warmth of friendship.

The Palestinians are dying.

I've been meditating for many years, and I live in peace, in the quiet
of the country.

Their children's blasted bodies lying broken on the streets.

I don't have much money, but I have a home and it's warm and
there's food in the kitchen and I'm content—except

They're performing surgeries without anesthetic, without hospitals,
without medications, without hope.

And though I cannot help it, I am complicit, so I give it what I can;
cradling it within me, between the lines, between rising and sleep.

Alexander Anlyan

Today's Horrorscope

You will have both arms
hacked off with a machete
by folks who don't like you.

You will be doused with gasoline
and set alight in a cage
by folks who don't like you.

You will have your head cut off
with a Bowie knife on a beach
by folks who don't like you.

You will get crushed
under fallen rubble after a bombing
by folks who don't like you.

You will be dipped, slowly,
into a tub of sulfuric acid
by folks who don't like you.

You will drown trying to repair
subsea cable equipment sabotaged
by folks who don't like you.

Your deli will be looted,
trashed, and burned
by folks who don't like you.

Your car will get hit
with an anti-tank rocket fired
by folks who don't like you.

Your friends will get slaughtered
in hand-to-hand combat
by folks who don't like you.

You will get knifed open
and get your organs cut out
by folks who don't like you.

You will get shot in the face
with a 12-gauge shotgun
by folks who don't like you.

Deluded, you will wish
for better times to come,
and you will be disappointed.

According to tomorrow's horrorscope,
things for you
will only get worse.

John Foy

I woke up thinking of them

those fifty left —
hostages in Gaza.
I thought how they must look,
no air or daylight
for four hundred thirty-seven days.
Nation leaders say release is near—
how agonizing though
must be these last days, days of hope –
maybe their kidnappers
will feed them well, let them wash
for sake of appearance
to the world
(whether they were treated that way or not).
But I see a near death-mask,
state of mind withdrawn, numb.
Will they be able to react to anything
once in the day's light?
I must have dreamt of them too
but can't be sure what was dream or wake.
I go to the Times hoping these thoughts
were premonitions. But again, nothing.
Maybe page 5 will say people are meeting
from the US, Qatar, maybe even Israel.

"Getting close" we're told
What is the dividing line
Between close and release?
What is the line between life
and no longer able to bear
the constant pain
of heartbreak and grief?
There is this, who happen to be
my flesh and blood, my kin.
But what of those who are other's kin,

their flesh, their blood?
Their homes become rubble
maimed and murdered children.
Al Jazeera shows bloodied bodies,
eyes round with fear.
We hear the bombs.
No one wants to look––
blood on our hands too.
A nightmare, it seems,
I can't wake up from.

Arlene Iris Distler
December 16, 2024

I Choke on Grace

Unmerited favor in a time of
casual genocide.
Each footfall of those
on a slow death March
from their devastated homeland
(to—where?)
grinds the blade of despair
deeper into my soul.
My heart limps along,
kicking rage down the road.
I would finish this poem
If I knew how.
Lord, have mercy.

Nikki Grimes

Candle

Hate
drips off
every word,
every deed,
every intention.
Evil
has been handed
the reins,
but the journey
will not end
in greatness
unless love leads.
Heed the call
to be a candle
in the darkness.
Only love
can unite us,
lift us,
save us.

Christine DePetrillo

Border Fugue

A border is unreal the way a god is unreal.
Even if it is a river
god demanding human sacrifices.

A god is real the way a border is real,
as real as the human beings sacrificing
all their savings just to wade across a river,

toddlers held above their heads
like sacrifices offered to a god with a holster.
A border dams a river of bodies,

damns a river of bodies
to stasis, to statelessness, just
unreal enough no gods need take them in.

Human sacrifices, packed in the back of a truck,
await the rite. Flashlights make
their big eyes glow like those of feral cats.

The god of borders is only as real
as the river that drowns you,
as the rifle that's found you

in the back of a truck, awaiting the night.
The real borders always river in the mind.
Kneel in a row before the god in a badge.

Amit Majmudar

The Snake

At the Save America rallies, after the damnation of the *criminal aliens breaking
across our borders* and *1,900 percent more murders*, he would ask the crowds
if he could read a poem. *This has to do with immigration*, he'd say. The crowds
would whoop and yip. He would read *The Snake*, words stolen from a song,
from the hand of a dead Black singer who could not snatch it back, a jazz fable
spun on vinyl, a tale from the fabulist of Greece centuries before Christ.

The crowds would listen to the poem: Bikers for Trump, Cops for Trump, Uncle
Sam in his beard, the Statue of Liberty in her crown, the millionaire who sells
pillows on TV. They would testify in T-shirts that said, *Jesus is My Savior, Trump
is My President*. They would hoist the Stars and Bars or signs that rhymed,
Trump 24 or Before. They would see the movie of the poem in their heads:

The snake frozen on the road, the woman scooping him up tight to nurse
him with milk and honey by the fire, the incandescence of his skin brought
back to life, the woman's kiss and the viper's venomous bite, her question
Why, then the words oozing from his tongue: *You knew damn well I was a snake
before you took me in*. The crowds would howl at the moral, at the punch line,
at the *tender woman* who would die of tenderness. Like a preacher spelling
out the lesson of a parable, their president would repeat: *Immigration*.

As they slept—the bikers and the cops, Uncle Sam and the Statue of Liberty,
the millionaire on his magic pillow—adolescents from Guatemala scalded
the killing floors at the slaughterhouse in Grand Island, Nebraska, their hoses
like snakes spewing rivers that bubbled in the steam. Around them, the blades
of skull splitters and bone saws waited for their fingers to slip, fangs lurking
in the murk of early morning, in the daze behind the goggles on the faces
of adolescents from Guatemala, sleeping the next day at Walnut Middle School,
shaken awake by teachers who spotted the acid burns on their hands.

Martín Espada

Aunt Esther

for Esther Beckman (1883-1973)

She's eighty-nine and fondly remembers the Lunts
and the carousel, ducks on the lake in the park.
It's August '72, sweltering, and Esther's
reading *The Catcher in the Rye* for the first time.
Outside, it's dusk and street lights flicker,
alarms are going off, sounds of breaking glass.
"He's doomed," she says, looking up from her book.
"The grown-ups in this story all love death."
Years later, tonight, they're back, they're visiting,
she's here with Holden, and they want to talk.
Illegal children, cages, madden them.
"And vanishings," she says, "it's even worse."
They're shouting, and the pavement wants to burn.
A few at the corner stare, some nod, as we turn.

Stephen Bluestone

Seed Shock

We stamp our feet as we come in, but snow clings
and melts in puddles by our chairs during the class, drying too,
before we finish and leave.

Bisnu is late, scrapes into her place, tossing puffs of icy gusts
that fresh up our minds.

Even Minh, madly lovely, blinks at these tufts of cold
and looks around, catches my eye and smiles.
I encourage her to speak, but no, just the smile.

I am here with them in their first winter, to offer words and witness.
I bring them dried cayenne — from my garden, I tell them —
because Lachi has told me of the food they miss from home.

Ganesh tells me they will not cook with these peppers
but split them and plant the seeds. Noted.

Minh did not lose her home.
She knows where it is, and who took it, maybe one at a time.

Her insides shocked, torn and scrambled by people,
maybe just one at a time. She knows.

Her body, here,
listens to our nonsense sounds as a soothing lullaby.
She smiles readily and is deeply wrapped, there.

Yet the fresh breeze moved her. I smile back
and hope she wants to speak someday.

Eva Zimet

Subtext

You fit the description, they said.
You describe our worst fear—a free Black man
walking like he belongs here, like here belongs to him,
like he has rights, like he knows it.
The description of the suspect, they said.
You are—your Black body suspected
of enticing our women, of subverting our power structures,
of daring to move through the world, our world.
Put your hands where we can see them, they said.
Put your politics where we can tokenize them,
put your protests where we can weaponize them,
put your women where we can objectify them,
put your children in schools where we can ghettoize them.
You're not the right guy, they finally said.
You're not the right guy to feed the prison industrial complex today;
you're not the right guy to be in our club, where we wear
our privilege openly, white as any bedsheet; you're not the right guy
to question our right to yank you out of your life to play our game.
You're free to go, they said.
You're free to carry this trauma forward in your body;
you're free to blame yourself when its tendrils trip you;
you're free to resent us, but never to unleash your frustration
because you have only your tongue and we have the guns.;
you will never be free as long as we are on duty,
as long as we dutifully detain you, the modern way to chain you.
Go on, before we change our minds, they said.

Aria Dominguez

Shouldering

The dream bird father sitting on my shoulder
is singing in my ear: *Now that you're older*
than I was when I left the rocky road,
it is your turn to shoulder the load,
answer questions students need to ask.
You are an elder now. You wear the mask
of wisdom. So you tell them
Tell them what?

The song breaks off. In somebody's back seat,
a baby. Whose? More babies on the border.
Terror, desperation, rage. Disorder
of crowded house, tap leaking, family,
students leaning in to question me:
Where should we go now? Tell us what to do.
The road's uphill, and that is all I know,
borrowing, burrowing, stirring the dark stew,
blended broth of night visions and day,
instructions garbled, watchmen standing tall
and menacing at gates along a wall.
Gaps in the rampart: raw red border zone.
Children wake and cry along the line.
The students' questions pound relentlessly.
Dream father, bird of omen, oh tell me –
the lost, the hungry, the abandoned—who
will take care of them? The grownups knew
the answers to these questions. And now
we are grown up, whose job is it to know?
The reassuring elders, where are they?
The dream bird looks at me and hops away.
Always uphill the steep road poetry
Scattered syllables still in my ear
when I sit up and the red world is here.

Rachel Hadas

Child at the Wheel

Trees smear by
women land

on the windshield
giraffes in the rearview

a single wheelchair
breaks the glass

bees fly in
it takes everything he has

to stay on the road
with such small hands

he signs his name
and wads up the woods

then turns
toward the coast

steps on the gas
for all it's worth

until the curve
until the cliff

until the wind
until the Earth

Wyatt Townley

Baby Hitler

That's what they used to tell you, when you said
you hated someone: *You only think that, dear,*
because you don't know the whole story.
We're all innocent out of the gate.

So I pictured newborn Adolf, no fürer, no 'stache,
no boots to click together, like shiny castanets.
Just a helpless infant, all spindly legs and
pale arms splashed with blue veins.

I tickled his tummy, looked into his shining eyes,
and saw the future there, trains crowded with
families and children who were too brown,
too full of life, to be allowed to live.

Now it's all happening again, the anger, the stony hate.
Because another babe's come of age, moving so fast
we can't count, won't miss, the ones who are
spirited away, locked up, killed off.

Again, I need to split in half, give myself two hearts—
one to nurture and support a frightened child,
and one to loathe the evil he's grown up
to unleash on you and me,
                   on our whole,
                            astonished world.

Louise Hawes

The Ministry of Frost

January, 2017

Never by human agency appointed,
the secret Minister that decked this town
with snow, swathing white houses and white acres,
hangs racks of silver pens, their sharp points down.
Though some are by protesting blasts disjointed,
and falling, spear through skin to icy bone,
enough still cling, perfected, for their maker's
enactments. His hard laws are all well known,
but very few of them are understood.
There is no loving hand in his decision
to send us to or save us from the slaughter
of wind and ice and hunger. Marks for good
and bad are all erased with white precision.
He signs his silent name in shining water.

Meredith Bergmann

Loss of Intrigue

Plato's Republic found opened to Book VIII *in a garbage heap during the fifth week of a garbage strike.*

I never read the book. Already tattered, it was opened and bent to the page
saying *For we cannot suppose States are made of oak and rock.* Solid,
in other words. Given the backdrop of back-up up and down the street, intrigued,
I read on: *ourselves* made out of gold, silver, bronze, and ore, in that order,
to illustrate how mixing of races would reverse, degrade into *inequality*
and irregularity resulting in *hatred and war.* A little too close to the present
and trending authoritative government's very obvious purge for racial purity
and control of wealth, I didn't need to say garbage. I could lean the other way
and shout, Stop the strike! My excuse? I was still adjusting to a new world order.
Across the street, a tossed plastic space monster's red eyes switched on/shorted
out. A toy fire truck sat next to it, axles splayed. Someone grown too big sat on it;
at the same time, could be so small: the ladder was extended, but every rung split.
Mr. Big climbed into Plato's world ending conflagration or escaped out. Or
suggested a broken helix, a genetic junk offering. Plato's *aberration*, but my *Well
now, we're still here* no longer cut it.

Scott Withiam

Rain or Shine

When a son cries, his tears flow out of his mother.
When a daughter cries, her father wipes his eyes.

When a nation cries, we all hurt. Earth rains.
Sun shines. We, the people, vote.

We choose who gets elected.
Rain or shine, we are all connected.

James Bird

Americans in Love

Is sainthood all
you thought it would be

Don't butter-
coat it, Braxton!

        *   *

How quietly traffic
impresses its will
upon nature.

By the way,
we overshot the trattoria.

        *   *

Words once piercingly
beautiful—now rote.

Here's an open heart,
Here's a crisp $100 bill,

        *   *

Eyesight becomes language:
stemware
        cilantro
            chanterelle

Mike Puican

Hotel Mar-a-Lago

after The Eagles

On a dank Palm Beach island, Aqua Net in my hair,
Warm smell of a Big Mac rising up through the air;
Up above on my flat screen, Fox News shimmering bright,
My mood grew heady and my mind grew dim, I settled in for the night.

KFC, Little Caesar's, or maybe Taco Bell,

And I was thinkin' to myself, "Why not all three, what the hell!"

Then they brought me a milkshake, on a gold-plated tray,

If lackeys enter from the corridor, I smile at them and say,

    "Welcome to the Hotel Mar-a-Lago,

    Such a lovely place (such a lovely place),

    Such an orange face.
    Plenty of room at the Hotel Mar-a-Lago;
    If you kiss my rear (if you kiss my rear),

    You can hang out here."

Melania's recently shifted primary residence,
She's in New York now with our pretty boy, 'cause she's got sense.
Now it's Vance in the courtyard, sweet parasite—

But Vance must remember, he could be gone overnight.

So I called up Mike Johnson, said "Hey, give me my way;"
He said, "You haven't needed Congress since Inauguration Day."

And still, Vlad Putin is calling from far away,

Wants my help in the middle of the fight, longs to hear me say,

    "Welcome to the Hotel Mar-a-Lago,

    Such a lovely place (such a lovely place),

    Such an orange face (such an orange face).

    We're givin' it up from the Hotel Mar-a-Lago,

    What a big surprise (what a big surprise)

    For our past allies."

Secrets we're revealing, with Diet Coke on ice,

And I say, "We are all just beautiful on an unsecured device."

And in the master bathroom, what I've hidden (none too soon),
They grab it—that damn FBI—but it turns out, I'm immune!
Last thing I remember, I was making up some lore,
I had to double down on lies I told the night before.

"Relax," said Steve Bannon, "We are programmed to deceive:

If you say it loud and long enough, they will all start to believe."

Thomas Schmidt

Spring:
The Way Things Were Up Until Now

Signs and Wonders

"If it is consistent, it is incomplete; if complete, inconsistent."
—Kurt Gödel

For it will come to pass
      that they live in Bakersfield
and the gardens of Coalinga,
      where they enter the rock

and live in the rock
      and remain in the rock when they die.
For their high-definition eyes
      are more than nature and art,

and the dust of their seeing
      paints them from within.
For they please themselves with images
      and images of images,

Their lips are stung by bees;
      their breasts yield no milk.
The miser lies down with the master,
      the skinny clerk with the fat.

For the land of plenty
      is the land of baristas?
For their sisters work at Walmart,
      and their unions are non-existent.

They prepare the table with Popeye's;
      fuel desire with lottery tickets;
and live forever
      downwind from the disaster.

Signs of trees but no trees;
        images of water but nothing clear to drink.
They burn at the sight of beauty,
        are reckless without cause,

rational without understanding.
        Among the owls and bats,
they hang from buildings and bridges,
        for nothing has been saved for the winter

and summer is but half constructed.
        The opossum dances with his mistress,
as the priest with his god;
        the rabbit with its mechanic,

as the needle with its habit.
        For a suckling child shall lead them
through the streets of Mexico City.
        Though the amusements are shuttered,

and the wind burns cold,
        the sands of Coney Island
shall be flames of amazement.
        For when their forests are bare,

a child will write them back into existence,
        one branch at a time,
until the wilderness fills with words
        and Gödel's theorem is enacted.

Gödel is consistent:
        how shall we incomplete him?
Gödel, Gödel, teakettle,
        what was the future today?

How can we be One,
        now that mastery's gone?
What rights must we wrong?
        What songs have we unsung?

(Isaiah)

Paul Hoover

The Way Things Were Up Until Now

I am bored of all the excuses.
Bored as Mayakovsky
at the Finnish painters' exhibition
barking like a dog through the foreign minister's toast
until he cried and sat down. Deadly serious.
I am bored as an elegy. I mean,
why care at all, speaking as a pitfall
in a world of pits. But we do. To the death.
We all agree to garden this year.
And my raspberry bushes,
picked over by wrens—
I'll make them great again
and let America go wild.
It'll be all trumpets and leeks and lilacs
from here on out.
Let's stop paying for it, get it free.
Let's plan our victory gardens to supplement grief,
boost morale, as though something new
and uncontrolled were available—
it is the original new hot future joy.
We're making it out of dough.
And the illusion of separateness,
let it go back into remission.
Just look at you—you look
like a resurrected child.
A serious drama in a cosmic joke.
Scarred, masked, dangerous.
And what of the new Eucharist?
How hungry I always am. How I long to lack.
Though in Walmart
my heart beats a little faster.
I want the world to heal up.
And the world is a field—as if it were indeed flat, curving
and caving, as if it were a piece of paper,

a Gustave Doré engraving
from the Divina Commedia,
the one with the silhouettes of Dante and Beatrice
standing in front of the blinding
exploding white rose
that you realize when looking more closely
is all made up of bodies and wings twisting together;
the "saintly throng," they call it, mashed and hurtling,
an image of Heaven, and the creation of angels, though it is
frenzied as any image of Hell, around a divine nipple,
Odin's lost eye in the well, the drain to the other side,
joy that gets more frantic
the more you try to quiet it down.

Bianca Stone

Sunday Morning Haiku

Sun touching each leaf,
churches arguing over
whose feet (not) to wash.

Mike Puican

"Ask What"

How can you fix this? sing the rusting spears
of the iron fence. We are coming for you.

What can you do? accuse the tax returns,
unfiled, and the condolences, unwritten.

What can you change? chuckle jars of pennies,
chock full of tiny silent presidents.

Who can you help? persist the yellowed headlines,
crumpled in heavy crates of family junk.

Where can you have an impact? worries the axe,
stuck in the ceiling. You need to look sharp.

How much can you send? demands the screen,
its glass withholding everything you want.

When can you speak up? whispers the poem,
collected scat of years of muttering.

Meredith Bergmann

What We're Not Supposed to Say

> *"The flocke goeth to wrecke and vtterly perisheth."*
> —Ephraim Udall 1548

I swear by the "mighty woman with a torch"—
big trouble's brewing
when we're not supposed to say
fetus   female   fluoride,

or the no-no *bird flu   peanut allergies   elderly   uterus,*

two hundred fifty words
verboten,
erased from the federal lexicon,

I tell you, the merry-go-round's off its rocker,
the music rank and roily.

Reader, it crossed my mind—
We need drums.

Lots of drums:
bodhráns, udus, tablas, come-together-in-solidarity drums,

drums to enhance cognitive function
and soothe our sorry souls,

when every word and every thing is again possible,
and for God's sake
when *they/them she/he you and I*
reestablish justice for all,

and yes, oh, definitely, unequivocally yes—
wipe clean the fools on the hill.

Pamela Ahlen

What Am I Waiting For?

(with apologies—and thanks—to Lawrence Ferlinghetti)

I am waiting for the Clark Street bus, always late.
I am waiting for the towers to fall and spring back,
        "a renaissance of wonder."

I am waiting for the green morning's green new deal
        to come, for peace to ever
        be real.

I am waiting to believe in peace, for all I've ever
        seen is war—on TV, yes, but still
        assault to innocent eyes.

I am waiting for my EV to charge.
I am waiting for somebody to do something.

I am waiting for USAID to bar the door.
I am waiting for Treasury officials to call the police.

I am still waiting,
        waiting for someone to do something.
Today or sooner, if you please!

I am waiting to remember
        what "waiting for wonder"
        means—now.

I am waiting for the Snow Moon
        to rise, bluing the snow,
        planets trailing it
        across the sky.
Will that be wonder?
        Or its Wikipedia definition?

I am waiting for our trees to fall,
        loggers to carry them away,
        lumber for houses
        for homeless children.

I am waiting for politicians
        to learn that we all
        yearn for home,
        for wonder.

I am waiting for everyone
        to acknowledge their family
        of LGBTQ+ children.

I am waiting for love
        of learning, for schools
        to educate about civic life,
        teach the ABC's of protest.

I am waiting for agape,
        for cares and woes
        to wash away.

I am waiting to wake at 3 a.m. without anxiety.
I am waiting to wake at 4 a.m. to blue moonlight
        on snow. I am waiting
        to remember wonder.

I am waiting to believe
        a spring will come again
        when other countries
        will welcome us again.
I am waiting for justice,
        but even more for mercy,
        and waiting, oh so impatiently
        for wonder.

Sharon Darrow

Blues

May, 2020

Great cities flare: another unarmed black man killed by police,
but the *thin blue line*—what else?— is drawn to contain the resulting tumult.
Meanwhile, as daylight dies in Vermont, I nod on my couch, remote
from mayhem and fury—retired and rich, ashamed of my own comfort.

And yet, barely conscious, my mind begins to stray from metaphoric
blues to sensible ones, like the wetland iris I behold each morning;
the blue sulphur butterflies, close to the ground, here again with spring;
the indigo bunting last week at our feeder, miraculous in its gleaming;

or "Blue Monday" as rendered so long ago by the late Fats Domino,
first record I owned—to think of which is to weep, I'm uncertain what for.
No, I know. The thrust of time. My bourgeois woes are as common
and small as much that I notice. This May, for instance, wild violets galore!

You see. Little things like that. The darkness will shroud the landscape in minutes
and certain creatures will search around for such refuge as they may come on,
while others prepare to wreak their blood-doused violence, although it's wrong
to talk that way. They do what predators do, whereas we humans…

Far off, there's a wailing train, a sound that has prompted art of a kind
I dearly love. You know what kind I mean. And of course there's the sky:
as its color recedes, I remember a grandchild clad entirely in blue.
Last fall. It was Halloween. She *was* the sky. From her father she gets

the African blood for which I pray to whatever God I can summon
she won't have to suffer. I shiver. I try to will back one of my trances.
I can't make it happen. I ache to dream an assuaging blue forever.
I'd paint the world. But whom do I think I help with poetical fancy?

I hear through a screen the beginning hoots and screams. Then dark takes over.

Sydney Lea

"Here pity only lives when it is dead"

> *"Qui vive la pietà quand' è ben morta."*
> —Dante, Inferno 20.28 (Mandelbaum translation)

Here pity only lives when it is dead.
Here, to be pitiless is piety.
Here cruelty, deemed Christianity,
Is praised whenever bitter tears are shed.

Here stands a woman in designer jeans
And baseball cap before a crowd of men
Who with shaved heads are caged inside a pen.
Power is what she seeks by any means.

The great barbarian in all his glory
Applies perfume to cover up his stench.
Discovered in his lies he doesn't blench.
Here truth is merely spectacle and story.

Old men who do the bidding of the king
Give trillions to the rich—and which is worse,
They rob the indigent without remorse
Of health, of education, everything.

Their only interest is short-term gain,
Fomenting xenophobia, spreading lies.
Whether the forests burn or floods arise
To inundate the cities of the plain,

Whether we breathe in deadly toxic fumes
And plastic chokes the creatures of the sea—
This isn't their responsibility.
Catastrophe on the horizon looms.

He levies tariffs, calls for their repeal
On the same day. Either he's unaware
That this breeds chaos or he doesn't care.
He is the boss and wants to make a deal.

Even our friends have now become our foes.
He thinks Canadians must be so dumb
That they would put themselves under his thumb.
He calls the shots; therefore, anything goes.

He and his henchman, a like-minded thug,
Berate the heroic leader of Ukraine
On television, treat him with disdain.
They raise his hopes up, then they pull the rug

From under him. It's all a cruel charade
To curry favor with his "base" and send
Greetings to Comrade Putin, his dear friend;
Also, to demonstrate that foreign aid

No longer sorts with US policy.
It's all become so sordid, has it not?
It goes against the grain of what we thought
Was possible or that we'd ever see.

Now he embraces cryptocurrency,
A boon for drug lords, money-laundering crooks,
To keep their filthy lucre off the books—
People who lack all sense of decency.

Those who arrived from some beleaguered shore,
Who labored in the fields in the hot sun,
Doing the work we never would have done—
Sudan awaits them or El Salvador,

If he should have his way, this cruel man.
What if our better inclinations fail
And he and his cruel minions should prevail?
What would it mean to be American?

His cruelty impels him; he is drawn
By childhood furies to be pitiless.
Lawless himself, he's bent on lawlessness.
Lawless, ungoverned fury drives him on.

Henry Weinfield

All That Life

after a long walk

window-ledge perched,
a just-fledged sparrow

trills her freedom, voice
opera-house strong, head hairs

the same white gossamer as
a bridge-web, a dream-catcher,

two kayakers below padding down-
stream in non-deport luxury,

unlike a skunk to oblivion,
pregnant belly, bright pink teats

exposed in a surround of traffic,
her slumber as permanent as

a Gazan from hunger, no leaf-loam
burial for all that life, yet

a baby snapper, eyes fisted shut,
lost on unpuddled asphalt,

allows a scoop, a portage
to water shallows where eyelids

lift in an aria of relief

Elizabeth Fred

Passover Poem of Pain—Gaza

This Passover I won't light the prayer candles,
Make the foods symbolic of the flight from Egypt,
flight from slavery to freedom
No, there is nothing to celebrate
For the Israelites, as they were called
in Biblical times, are lost—wandering
in a moral desert, even more than when
Moses found his people
worshipping a golden calf. Moses, angry,
called them a "stiff-necked" people—stubborn,
not comprehending this profound undertaking.
This sin is even more egregious.
How many drops taken from the wine glass
Will it take to atone this sin? What will it take
for the stubborn, unseeing of Israel to awaken?
To hear the words of the Almighty, the prophets,
given to them? Thou shalt have no other G-d
before me—not even land.
Will the people, my people,
finally yield to the spirit of love and compassion,
bend to the law of love.

Arlene Iris Distler

Get Here

Get here however you can, drive 'til the barricades stop you then jump out and run, one shoe in each hand, the soles of your feet numb to the gravel, the glass, numb like your brain, your chest, come, witness this train wreck of a country where back to school means back to bloodshed, come, scan the crowd for your precious baby, eye the others still waiting, watch as the children speak into microphones of playing dead to survive, listen to how they sound like seasoned adults, innocence in this country reserved solely for newborns, watch as they're the ones to console their crying parents, these beautiful souls always on edge, on guard, always ready to drop to their knees, to lay atop a friend, to pray as the gunshots ring out around them, all so that you can have your precious guns, tell me, tell *them*, is it worth it?

Amy Allen

The Still Small Possibility

"*Hope is action.*"—Grace Paley

Any day now
news will bend
like cosmos stems
toward the sun,
marches will
render questions
safe to ask,
considered,
as tongues turn
from intimidation,
prayer flags sailing over
wide circles of children
mourning another friend's
death, compelled to accept

a republic of guns
like chewing gum
stuck to pockets of those
profiting from fear,

when a stanza can speak
to the inner peace
of gathering cosmos seeds,
in refusing to name
a corporation human,
a brother enemy
a sister voiceless
a child defenseless,
offering soup on streets,
stories at the general store,
arresting what war we can
in verses spoken
from a woman's wide lap
long after she's gone.

Judith Janoo

Abject Cruelty

is all I can say
about what is going on now
rancorous decisions made by billionaires
meant to marginalize millions
immigrant refugees try their best
to follow everchanging rules
meant to keep them out
far from polite society
incapable of owning property
forced to relocate constantly
meant to separate wheat from chaff
keep white supremacy alive
but who will do all the work necessary
to keep the country running
certainly not the billionaires
whose disrespect for workers is palpable

Sandy Edmonds

Tanatofobia: Fear of Losing Your Mexican Mother

1982, the year our mother died.
We'd been prepared to leave her side
but not this way. We'd lose her to—la migra then; today, el hielo, ICE.
She, a leader for the packinghouse strike.
She, without papers, with one fist held high
as workers shouted *¡Huelga, ¡Huelga!* into night's
muggy air. The stars amused by such a sight:
women standing tall and energized
for a change, after weeks of lumbering, weary-eyed,
to the parking lot at quitting time.
My brother upset he never heard her come home, or rise
at dawn to get to work again. I did, once or twice.
Enough to see this labor eating up the light inside
her. She, fading into darkness as her shadow cried.
I told my brother that this fight
was giving our beloved overburdened Mami life.
We did our part as well, scribbling a sign
that read: FAIR HOURS, FAIR PAY.
But Papi also warned us on that day
that agriculture bosses liked to sway
power in their favor. The men in green, or gray,
would come to drag the picketers away.
The union's victory, however, meant that Mami got to stay
forever. Imagine, then, our great surprise
to see a man in black entering the doorway.
A voice like doves colliding midflight.
A mustache like a pair of scythes,
one curving left, the other to the right.
No medicine, no magic prevented her demise.
Cruel death. It hollows home and heart and boyhood face
of Mami love. No surrogate can fill that empty space.
But at the packinghouse, another swiftly took her place.
Time heals, Papi said. RIP, 1982. We waved goodbye
forever. Until the fear of losing Mexican mothers was revived
in 2025.

Rigoberto González

The Iguanas Skitter Through the Cemetery by the Sea

Viejo San Juan, Puerto Rico

The iguanas slither from the branches of trees splintered by the hurricanes.
The iguanas crawl from the cracks in the ground split by the earthquakes.
The iguanas rise from brown floodwaters that carry bridges to their doom.
The iguanas multiply through the night of blackouts in hospitals and morgues.
The iguanas burrow beneath roads to bury their eggs in the lungs of cities.
The iguanas slap their clawed feet as they churn the earth of the farmer's field.
Iguanas rip the rough skin of mango; iguanas rip banana; iguanas rip papaya.

The iguanas skitter through the cemetery by the sea, tails snapping when
they disappear between the crosses, sunning themselves on the walls,
hiding in the crevices of crypts where families still cling to each other
beneath the weathered stone. The iguanas stare stupefied at the bust
of a mustachioed poet who died after the bacteria feasted on his heart.
The iguanas know nothing of José de Diego, his songs of the guaraguao
and the pitirre, the hawk fleeing from the two-ounce kingbird, the slash
of claws to save her young still blind in the nest. The poet's hawk is *long
and dark with imperial wings*, the poet's kingbird *an arrow through the neck*.

An iguana warms his belly on the flat stone that says *Pedro Albizu Campos*.
The iguanas know nothing of Albizu: the lawyer and the canecutters' strike,
the crowd listening in the rain, cane stalks in their heads igniting like torches.
The iguanas learn nothing from El Maestro, his staccato tongue on the radio
splitting the ground under the boots of the military governor, collapsing
the courthouses and flagpole of empire. The iguanas keep vigil at the tomb,
burial stone white as the stone of *seditious conspiracy* that buried him, stone face
of thirty years' incarceration, subversive tongue gone to stone after the stroke.
The iguanas forget the thousands in black sweeping his coffin to the edge of the sea.

The green of the iguanas in the cemetery is the green of soldiers in uniform.
The green of the iguanas in the cemetery is the green of felt at the casinos.
The green of the iguanas in the cemetery is the green of cash on cruise ships.
The green of the iguanas in the cemetery is the green stacked in steel vaults.
The green of the iguanas in the cemetery is the green of lawn after lawn hidden
by gates, the green of mangoes in a bowl on every table of the absentee landlords.

In the movies on the drive-in screens and Saturday matinees of the Cold War,
iguanas played the dinosaurs, horns glued to their snouts, frills pasted to their
heads, thrashing in closeup struggle with other iguanas over *The Lost World*.
The dead eyes of the iguanas, keeping vigil over the city of the dead, will never
see the asteroid of their extinction, the earth melting to suck their bones into
whirlpools of mud, the wave sweeping them to sea, the flight of the poet's kingbird.

Martín Espada

Corrido del ciclista

Pedalea Andrés por el sendero
Llega a la ciudad
Al downtown de la ciudad
Pa' construir andamios
Pa' limpiar un parking lot
Para entregar comida
En la oficina del Chase Bank

Pedalea Andrés
Hasta cruzar el puente
El puente de la Michigan
En la esquina con Wacker Drive

¿Y qué encuentra Andrés
Al cruzar el puente?

El hielo fétido
Que en domingo
invade la ciudad
El downtown de la ciudad
El puente de la Michigan
Esquina con Wacker Drive

Pedalea Andrés
Hasta mirar el hielo
El fétido hielo
Que en domingo
invade la ciudad

Andrés pedalea y grita
"I'm not a citizen but I am"
"I'm not a citizen but I am"

Y el hielo persigue al inmigrante
Y el hielo persigue al inmigrante

Pedalea Andrés por el sendero
Quiere tocar el río
Y volverse pavimento
Y volverse todo viento
Pedalea y ya es viento.

Y el hielo no encuentra al inmigrante
Y el hielo no encuentra al inmigrante

Pedaliamos
Con Andrés por el 90
Por el 290 y la 55.

Y el hielo no encuentra al inmigrante
Y el hielo no encuentra al inmigrante

Raúl Dorantes

Corrido of the Cyclist

Andrés pedals down the road
Arrives in the city
In the city's downtown
To build scaffolding
To clean a parking lot
To deliver food
At the Chase Bank offices

Andrés pedals
Until he crosses the bridge
The Michigan Avenue Bridge
At the corner of Wacker Drive

And what does Andrés find
When he crosses the bridge?

The stinking ice
That on Sunday
Invades the city
The city's downtown
The Michigan Avenue Bridge
At the corner of Wacker Drive

Andrés pedals
Until he sees the ice
The stinking ice
That on Sunday
Invades the city

Andrés pedals and yells
"I'm not a citizen but I am"
"I'm not a citizen but I am"

And the ice goes after the immigrant
And the ice goes after the immigrant

Andrés pedals down the road
He wants to touch the river
And turn into pavement
And turn into wind
He pedals and now he's the wind.

And the ice doesn't find the immigrant
And the ice doesn't find the immigrant

Let's all pedal
With Andrés along I-90
Along I-290 and I-55.

And the ice won't find the immigrant
And the ice won't find the immigrant

Raúl Dorantes (translated by Mary Hawley)

Questionnaire

Where were you when you made the decision to sign up for ICE? When you signed the contract, did you think of your great-grandfather, the one who stowed away on that ship from France and leapt overboard in New York Harbor and swam to what he thought was freedom? Did you picture your brown niece, the one you taught to skateboard? Are you picturing her now, as you pull the mask up to your eyes? When you think of your grandmother as a child, fleeing the pogroms for life on the Lower East Side, do you remember how hard she worked? How young she died? When you think of your brown niece on the skateboard you taught her to ride, do you picture someone with a mask pulling her off it and zip-tying her hands? When you picture that, how do you feel inside? Where in your body do you feel whatever it is you feel when you remember the day your brown now-skateboarding infant niece came home from the hospital with your sister and her brown husband and they put her in your arms? When you think of your brother-in-law now, that brown man who taught you to play chess and helped you night after night with your math homework those years you lived with your sister and him because your father kept slamming you against the wall, do you picture someone in a mask yanking him from his car and slamming him to the ground? What do you plan to do with your $50,000 signing bonus? How many masks do you have at home? How often do you wash them? Do any of them have bloodspots? Do your stowaway grandfather and your pogrom grandmother appear as ghosts in your dreams? How much does a mask cost?

Alison McGhee

Hunger

I was born in the City of Dead
and died in the River of Children.
I am the infant smashed on the wall.
The kitchen is verboten!
The killers are insatiable for kalashnikovs.
Peshmerga, blood chief, my father.
Gulag, my mother, dirt soup.
I am yellow fever's young boy
run wild in poppy fields,
scorched. My broken finger,
am I to blame? My little cowlick?

Mary Meriam

To the Tune of "Veni redemptor gentium" by Ambrose of Milan

"D.H.S. Requests 20,000 National Guard Members to Help With Immigration Crackdown," by Hamed Aleaziz and Eric Schmitt, in New York Times, May 15, 2025

Not the schooner Adirondack
But the retired lightship Ambrose,
Not the mountains, their backtracks,
But the guardian saint of the coast,

The millions of us immigrants
Rode into harbor, found a home,
Discovered our deliverance
From the old T-Rex Syndrome.

The sandbars lifted from the way,
The fog was given eyes to see,
The Ambrose lanterns turned to day
The night of oceanic misery.

Into the silence of despair,
The Ambrose whistled allegro,
The message near and far declared
By the first lightship radio.

At the hour of our greatest need,
When greed swells to the fullest tide,
When hate flies at a lightning speed,
When insult rises up with pride,

Come, old friend, constant helper, mate,
Out of the museum and the dock,
Be born again with birth's prized freight,
The blessings of being our bedrock.

As your namesake was blessed by bees
Splashing his face with a honeyed drop,
A tear of the cloud, if you please,
Hailing the Hudson's long workshop,

Speak, Ambrose, sweetly speak once more
For the weary and the weak
From Senegal to Singapore:
You'll find the mountains that you seek.

Jee Leong Koh

Stand By and Listen for the Whistle

What are you doing in the name of God

Today dear Pastor of the Faith you claim

To run our world with   now that your sheep

Have outgrown their lambskins   good little dogs

Have grown up too   and look for any way to maim

For you   we'll sharpen our teeth on each Bo Peep

Now tell us another nursery rhyme that's true

Socially   what is your whim today   who speaks

Through your angels in attendance   we need meat

And someone who will bake our bread   will you?

We need to go out hunting with our claws and beaks

To go from starving dogs to wolves is no big feat.

This fire's been burning underneath for years

Thank God that you unleashed us from all fears.

JPayne

That Gritty, Bright, Shadowless Sunlight

That gritty, bright, shadowless sunlight
Of the early 40's, which caressed the blimping curves
Of subdued automobiles, shines weak and yellow
In this new century. How to refire the sun? Stoke
Its aged, sclerotic, and too swiftly slipping cold bulk?
There is no harness on the sun, the last feather
Has fallen to earth, moss grows on the temple.
The last lights of the race corner and flick
In the gathering dust while the Freeway sings,
And the kettle boils, and news keeps coming in
On the TV.

Ron Lay-Sleeper

Today, I Figured I Should Finally Get Rid

of my *HARRIS FOR PRESIDENT* 2024 t-shirt,

along with a garbage bag full of stuff
I've been working up the courage to finally let go:

>a pair of jeans I haven't fit into since college
>a sequin mini skirt from a braver time
>a sweater with the tag still on it
>etc
>etc
>etc—

and as I make the handoff to the woman in a bright orange vest
with bags under her eyes from eight months of sleepless nights,
asking herself

>why
>how
>what now
>what next, what could possibly happen   next,

I wonder who might next find themselves holding this shirt
this bit of naivety   this hot trend turned last season in a matter of

77,303,568   votes
>betrayals
>punches to the gut
>slaps across the face

up to their chest in the cramped fitting room mirror?

Perhaps a collector

of old things
of once used things
of never really mattered things

will snatch it up   hold it over their heads   yell *jackpot!*
and give it
one precious taste

of the victory   the safety   the hope   the we're going to be *okay*

that was promised
long gone stale in its threads.

Kauakanilehua Māhoe Adams

The Truth as Well

Vermont: roads, rivers do-si-doed.
Now water runs where once was road,

And Harry's Hardware Store's back room—
the plumbing department—is a flume.

The torrents passed. They will return.
On Greek islands, hillsides burn.

The sky is orange, dark, and dire.
Between the water and the fire

tourists wait till help arrives.
And others—babies, husbands, wives—

have for how many years now been
trapped in a hellish in-between:

war and drought and poverty
or—also unrelenting—sea.

The Aegean, Aeschylus wrote,
blossoms with corpses. He was right.

Blossoms: the scarlet of bee balm,
lavender hostas, dewy calm.

Not far from here, they're pitching tents
in cemeteries. It makes sense:

cheek by jowl a house/a tomb.
They've had to leave their motel room.

The pandemic is almost over.
Why should the state provide their cover?

Empty houses in every town;
nowhere for families to lie down.

*So distribution should undo
excess?* Gloucester in *Lear* hoped so.

Solutions seem out of reach.
Tourists huddle on the beach.

Under a bridge on the rail trail
a homeless man lives, *fierce but frail,*

barefoot and bearded, so they say.
Watch out for him. My thoughts segue

to this screened porch, the steady croon
of busy bees all afternoon.

Foxglove, hosta, and snake root—
tempting targets, tall and sweet

flowers the hummingbirds attack
avidly with their needle beak.

A hummingbird sideswipes a bee
and zooms away too fast to see,

its buzz in harmony with the bees.
The man emerges from the trees,

crosses Route Two, comes to a halt
in Marty's parking lot, asphalt

glistening with rain. And who is he?
Nobody knows his history.

The Muses help us poets tell
lies *like the truth, but the truth as well.*

Such was the poet Hesiod's claim.
The Muses spoke to him by name,

taught him a song to glorify
both what was and what would be.

*Would be...*now? What to celebrate?
Fire and flood and people wait.

Elemental apocalypse:
tourists are herded onto ships.

Migrants packed in a leaky boat
rock to and fro to stay afloat.

In the woods by the rail trail,
rain clouds lower, grim and pale.

Rivers and streams will overflow
once more. Where should the homeless go?

Under a bridge or in a park?
The days are shorter. It's getting dark.

Cemetery? Rail trail? No.
All these are against the law.

In tents donated by the state
the homeless hunker down and wait.

Flood and fire and ruination:
what will be our celebration?

Listening daily to the news,
I keep an ear out for my Muse,

who inspires us to tell
lies like the truth, but truth as well.

Rachel Hadas

Pandemonium

(The name Milton coined for the capital of Hell in Paradise Lost.)

Here is old king Midas of Phrygia.
His longing for lucre made him gold before his time.
Watch him break a tooth on a 24-carat chicken wing.
Choke on a Diet Coke. And, with a single fatherly embrace,
turn his daughter into a glimmering hat-rack.

The man with "the touch." The Master of Poor Choices.

Asked to judge a musical competition, he gets himself on the wrong side of
    Apollo,
who, in a fit of pique, gifts Midas the ears of an ass.
Tin ears: Apollo making a point.
Tin ear—hardly an asset in running a center for the performing arts.
Or a country.

Foreign emissaries arrive,
wretched,
hat in hand,
plagued by drought,
war,
betrayal.
"Hee Haw," says Midas.

Midas hides his floppy auricles under a Phrygian hat. Now, only his barber
knows the truth. And what dangerous knowledge that is...
The barber dares not tell a soul.

Trembling, he digs a hole

and between cupped hands, whispers,

"Midas has the ears of an ass!"

Then he quickly fills the hole up again, pats it down,

and silently weeps, havoc roiling around him—

The wild, unrestrained uproar of a tumultuous assembly

led by a braying ass, his head stoppered up with greed, tone-deaf to mercy.

Tim Wynne-Jones

Summer: You Think This is Hot?

As a Lion in Secret Places

> *"I was a derision to all my people; and their song all the day. . ."*
> —Lamentations 3:14-26 KJV

The Lord marked me as filthy;
I'm a smudge upon the wall,
The darkest part of the night,
obscurity of the painting,
The howl at the pit of the throat,
the blind pig, the wack job,
A dog yoked to its cart,
dragged when it can't run.

The people will not approach
but to herd me out of town,
I pity the bailiff who must touch
my flesh to beat me.
The bride will grant no kiss;
the groom spits at my feet.
Angelic children smite me;
their dog snarls at the door.

Yet once they sat on my knee,
asking, *what do you see, our prophet?*
I bleed for myself alone.
The gold I touch is dimmed;
the gifts I give are abandoned.

Mu-sick, mu-sick,
I hear a sick cat calling,
the music of scorn and
unsuccessful glamor.

My ribbons wear and fade,
threading the street.
The cup is broken;
the chalice will not bear;

Sticks and stones, rickets;
unbearable gods bear down.

People gape at the color
in a wall, any movement at all,
even an earwig traipsing
over a widening crack.

Lo, it is given: insects totter
in and out of our eyes;
money is for nothing
and jobs disappear;
the music will not sing;
the plow will not fold.

No memory and no return;
even the place names change.
No arrival, no contemplation;
the wave eats the shore.

For the land is captive
and so are its schemes.
The eyes of strangers cry:
lamentable, yes; contemptible, too;
But what can we tell you,
what could we ever do?
Will the wind cleanse us,
lovers befriend us?

For the chorus of innocence
murders the choir;
For the virgin soprano
runs away with some guy.

(Lamentations of Jeremiah)

Paul Hoover

Naming Light

Moonlight falls on the city like a name,
on a woman waiting for the bus. We
don't know who she is, the sorrow
she's feeling, her cold hands and feet.

In a faint light, we see the woman,
the street, a few cars, a boy with
his dog, someone walking fast, a family
across the street asleep in the park.

Mike Puican

Don't Worry

They come with signs

to protest
the side we think is doing
the better job.

Even in our small town
they organize.

They stand at intersections,
block bridges

in rain or snow or blistering
sun.
They wear black.
They wear white.

I drive past
and wonder

what's for supper.

Cindy Faughnan

Florida's Famous For:

There was an edge of fear under it even then—
cash poor as ever, we nursed the old Volkswagen
down the coast, walked rainy beaches, climbed
with stubbornly sandy feet into sleeping bags
at night. We felt fragile,

displaced: nobody knew our names, very far from
Northern home, branded "not one of us" the moment
we said good morning. Bad dreams, apprehension.
But I had promised the children we would visit
(at last) Disney World

so we brushed each other off, stood tall, signed up
to tour a condo development, saying "Grandpa will like
this view, this option," signing everything except
the contract, all for three precious half-price tickets
into the magic place

that all their classmates boasted about. Bottles of water
hidden in our pockets so the last dollars could
stretch to ice cream. Clutching each other's hands
staring at the height of a roller coaster, submitting
to dark tunnels, harsh music:

how many miles now from Disney's forced exhilaration
to the fenced cages of an Alligator Alcatraz—pain, I hear,
is inevitable but suffering is optional. It scared us,
that famous theme park. But at least (oh God) we
knew there was an exodus, an exit.

Beth Kanell

It disturbs me

It disturbs me to know
our president doesn't read,
can't sit still for long,
doesn't listen to others
who surely know more than he,
who is no "loser"
but a MAN: like some celluloid hero
for whom only the highest
superlatives apply
            and who alone has resolved
            five—or is it seven?—wars.

I imagine he has crafted his world
out of golf balls and gold
spray for hair and skin, expensive suits,
with at least one big beautiful
busty female by his side;
just as I suspect
he buys words the same
as CEOs and slick politicians
            (nothing much
            over two syllables).

I acknowledge our president
can at times be a strategist—
knows how to play
one side against another;
            to deflect,
            to distract,
            as he takes the pulse
            of almost half our citizens,
labels facts as false,
labels lies as truth,
thinks we should believe simply

because He said so—
        maybe even believes himself.

I am convinced our president hates
nature, has no feelings for
anything or anyone other than himself;
don't think he has ever

walked in the woods—
        no cellphone,
        no bodyguards
        to stave off conspiracies
        of nut-crazed squirrels
        and drones disguised as birds—
or watched with awe
an eagle soar, a blue whale breach
like a god from the deep.

It disturbs me to think
our dyspeptic commander-in-chief,
swollen on burgers and hubris,
is mad as a blue-eyed bull
in the china shop of government,
is crazy as a loon—
as the high-pitched jitter of
a pileated woodpecker
just as the sun is setting,
        going down
        like a drowning man
        and taking us with him.

Joyce Thomas

Wrecking Ball & the muskrats

When Wrecking Ball & the muskrats tore up to Washington DC, they were even more
corrupt than them righteous rioters on the 6th of January,

Their wreckage seen on main-scream t.v.: they locked out federal workers
for the sake of <u>their own </u>liberty.

They were so (hell) bent that Tammany Hall seemed straight.
They denied the right of speech,
declared no need to vote,
replaced diversity with perversity,
erased archives of the woke.

Governors Pritzker and Mills said "I'll see you in court."
Judges & AGs stood firm on the rule of law until
Wrecking Ball ignored them and flew deportees
to El Salvador, a foreign holding pen, paid for by us...

Then he turned into a damn international tariffist.

Others spoke out: Bernie, AOC, and Walz held
Town Meetings in red states where Republicans hid and cowered.
Cory filibustered for 25 hours.
Heather filled a blog, showing history held dialogue.
Comedians had loads of material—too surreal to think.
While Rachel spotlighted our fascist king.

Now, commoners have had enough
of billionaires raiding public funds,
not paying their fair share.
"Hands off our Medicare!"
the people shout.
"We'll take to the streets!!
Until Justice finds Peace."

daithi

Take to the Streets, February 15, 2003

"I wish I could shut up, but I can't, and I won't." —Desmond Tutu

Is it dangerous, my daughter asked
exiting the bus against ten-degree gusts,
walking Manhattan's Third Avenue,
dark casement awaking like Rembrandt
stroked the morning,
our numbers multiplying,
spilling into Second with neglected appeals.
                  Sure, we were all mad
after the attacks, shocked back,
but what had these people done?
Wives of firefighters waved banners: *No blood for Oil*,
businesspeople, blue-collared, poor, frayed, disabled,
babies in strollers, Grace Paley, Susan Sarandon,
Desmond Tutu. 9/11 Families for Peaceful Tomorrows,
Half a million strong, said the man behind us
as we merged onto First, *The reports will pinch it,*
     say we're hippies, lefties,
gut our numbers. His suit had ridden many buses—
they always turn down the volume.
The world marched that day
against a rampage that would
yield no chemicals or Al-Qaeda.
Those who've walked the street never again
see only pavement. *No*, my daughter later told friends,
It isn't dangerous to walk,
only to not say a word.

Judith Janoo

No Kings

Winter went on forever.
Spring also went on and on forever.
Our world changed, fell screaming into forever.
Today is June 18 and this day is going on forever.
I am discontented, discombobulated, and I may be forever.
We who have realized we are patriots and have been forever
weep aloud in the morning, silently at midnight, call upon Forever
to save us. Forever says, "You must save yourselves, now and forever."
Tomorrow, no more weeping; tomorrow, new ways to resist, to ask, How long
will we oppose the liar who wants to be a king? Now and forever, forever and a day.

Sharon Darrow

On the way to the protest

"You can't be neutral on a moving train." — Howard Zinn

we stopped at the MFA
to get out of the heat of the train
to remember our humanity
to bring it with us

I went immediately
to the impressionist room
sat with Mary Cassatt's
young mother and child

girl at the morning table
washing, half dressed
getting ready for her day
my compatriot

sat with Gauguin's
where do we come from?
who are we?
where are we going?

and simply breathed…
later, after hours
under the hot sun
police on horseback

in a sea of chanters
we stayed within lines
that circumscribed us
lest we be arrested

although a few of us planned
to be dragged away
and were
we return to the cool

MFA to rest
next week
we will come again
to the salon

to the street
soul fed
to see, be seen
hear, be heard.

Joanne M. Giannino
June 19, 2024

Rising

There are a million of us—post-menopausal women
living middle-class lives. We not only know better
than our parents but better than our children.

I protested wars, marched for women's rights, and bucked Nixon.
No sit-com watcher, I listen to NPR, turn off fake news,
turn up Notorious RBG—she was one of us.

I buy organic and spend an extra buck for better wine.
And I can still dance a get-down, swivel hips to Motown
and wear you out on the floor.

I oh-oh-oh with good sex and am beyond faking orgasm.
I lust after younger men but prefer the patience of a seasoned one
and I still like to kiss.

So don't ignore us. We've got something to say,
And you'd better pay attention.
There are millions of us and we are rising

Marching, voting,
buzzing in one
gray swarm.

Louella Bryant

Fierce Compassion

You won't tame me! Wild thing; Woman.
I refuse to be de - moral - ized
      by your black-tar robes, your
          pens of pomposity
             the swings of your metaphorical
          gavels
       aimed at
          my abdomen.

I won't fall in to walk your chain-maiden line
no matter how many
      pasty-faced
          old white-men shuffle
             in their soft slippers
          hasten to sign
     diabolical decrees
          on the shrine.

I won't kneel.
No matter how many
      devout
          misguided Bible-thumpers
             shake their
          gold chain-crosses
     and moan
          their doctrines out.

For I am the Original Goddess. We are the Women
      of Ancient Times. We hold
          the Power of Transformation
          the Seeds
          in our Bellies.

We, the Women—Earth's Designated
        Beautiful Goddesses
        Know how
        to Bring
        the Magic
        of Fierce Compassion
        Unwavering Justice
        to Light.

Amabel Kylee Síorghlas

Frog

He started up again early in the spring—
the frog who lives in my tiny pond.
Not even a pond, really, just a
four-foot moat around a fountain.
Not much of a domain, but apparently
enough for someone so small.
All spring, all summer, he kept up his chant,
louder when the dogs barked or the
lawn mower roared. I don't know if he was
declaring his right to this bit of the world
or if he was looking for love. I suppose,
like the rest of us, a bit of both.
All I know is that I love this scrap
of a being who is so determined not to
let it go. Blessed are the small
and indomitable and unremittingly loud.

Lynn Ungar

Fire and Flood and Bureau Drawer

The Water Andric, once a slender thread
flowing clear and brown, is now a flood,

white water carrying downed trees along.
The Sheep Dip, once a swimming hole, is gone.

Over in Montpelier, canoes
paddle past the Capitol. Confused

cows in a bedroom; trout in a bureau drawer.
The rains let up. And then it rained some more.

The rushing water had no place to go;
creatures and crops alike lost in the flow.

Carrying her dog to safety, she
lost her footing, slipped, was swept away.

Relentless power of water on the move,
as strong as gravity, stronger than love.

More and more the elements conspire,
confronting us with water or with fire.

From Rhodes to Maui, a thin strip of sand
to huddle on, with death on either hand;

and migrants setting sail to hoped-for lives
pack into boats, are swallowed by the waves.

What's the best vantage point? From where can we
get a perspective on humanity?

Find a safe place, Lucretius writes, and you
see struggling people—it's a splendid view.

Pythagoras too, a passenger on cloud,
saw mankind as baffled and afraid.

Some of us help our neighbors in the flood,
after the fire, as we always did.

Love and dread, the known and the unknown.
We try to live as we have always done.

How long can we go on living this way?
Is it too late, as fire and water say?

This house sits on a hill; we've had good luck.
Still, windows, doors, and bureau drawers are stuck.

Having tugged a faded T-shirt out,
I breathe in layers of memories: summers, sweat,

and sunshine—fragrance fainter than the mold
or mildew (these shirts, like me, have grown old)

of winters in this empty house whose cold
rises like a specter from each fold.

Rachel Hadas

The Perfect Space

Writing poetry is a good hiding place
From the horror, the mayhem,
And the cruelty—
We foist on one another.
I pull a black drape
Over news I don't want to see
But I force my eyes
To open some nights to see
Empty-bellied children
With glassy eyes
Silent babies, lying listless
In a mother's arms—
A mother who can no longer cry
Having squeezed out the last drops
Hours ago.
Slowly—
I return to my laptop. Search for the perfect word
To fit in the perfect space.

Madeleine May Kunin

Shoelaces

I keep tying and untying my shoelaces
splitting hairs over definitions
in the absence of meanings
like little dolls bundled preterm
on the hospital floor
cold like the memories of tortured pasts
genocide, holocausts
8 million then now unimaginable
to the point of forgetting
where we came from
why we are here

Steve Minkin

Rhapsody on a Line by Poe

Is there a bomb in Gilead? And are
They flush with Kalashnikovs in Tel Aviv?
I visited a city on the *qui vive*,
Aquiver, ever on the eve of war.

Is there a consulate in Jerusalem?
I climbed in Kevlar up the Temple Mount;
I'm no religion, so it didn't count,
But given visions in the realms of REM,

I slept on Jesus, slept on Moses, slept
On every sura that assured me heaven
For fear I would awaken AK-47s.
I visited the Weeping Wall and wept.

There are too many one true Gods to worship.
I fished in Galilee and hooked a warship.

Amit Majmudar

Contradiction

Abortion opponents are stalking the land
taking personal freedom in the name of God
and the innocent child.

They care not for those who have suffered Rape or Incest.
They care not for the mother whose life is in peril.
They care not there's no money to put food on the table,
They care not that children grow up homeless on the streets.

It's the old biblical Creed of populating the Earth at all cost.
Old white men must have dominion over all within their reach.
It's the Church setting policy, enacting laws, for us.

Every life is precious, every life must be protected at all cost, they say.
And yet we have no care for those killed in mass shootings.
Children seem to have no right to a safe childhood without
guns exploding in their bodies at school.

The right to an AK-47 Trumps the lives of those it kills.
Woe betide those who would stand between
a man and his weapon of mass destruction.

But it is seldom the child of a politician gunned down.
They pay lip service to our loss but protect the NRA at all cost.
Our children are not protected from gun violence in their schools
But we must protect a fetus in the womb at a mother's expense.

We have no desire to protect those already here, already dear.
We offer impotent prayers and our hearts weep for the victims' families
because we know that it could be our son, our daughter.

Is it that we protect the fetus, to create more children just to be gunned
    down every day?

Mary Cheyne

Jus Soli

Pre-pill, and pre-the safe and legal
termination of unwanted pregnancies,
high school girls succumbed to their
boyfriends' desires with mixed feelings

and for up to a month after. *He said he pulled out.*
Young stomachs twisted into tight knots
over those next up to 28 days, until
an inkling of cramps (Oh, cramps! Rejoice!).

The same nerves light up after a cop
standing over his radar gun, points at you
giving you a chance to pull over before he mounts
his motorcycle and begins the chase. It doesn't take

long to calculate his response timeline. It's your
choice. Pick freeze, pull over, plead ignorant
and pay the fine or pick flight and get down
to the business of taking tight corners. You make

the decision. Jus soli credentials offer ways out
if caught, for your kind. There have always been
options. Imagine now, all the undocumented workers
in our country, suffering in fear for themselves, for

their children, daily. Let us forgive our immigrant
brothers and sisters for their trespassing, for choosing
life over death for their families, for choosing jobs
and safe streets around their homes and school and work.

Let us save whole families from the consequences
of decisions we will never have to make.

Nancy Stewart

In Thinking

a little more and then some more while cutting the grass today
about Donald Trump and his rise to power, I realized that despite
his towers, his golf courses, his gold, and his empire, that he'll
always be a felon with a dearth of decency and honor with no idea
of how to think or govern with any ability to weigh and consider or
conduct himself with civility. That he lives in what the philosopher,
Soren Kierkegaard, called an "acoustic illusion", which is no less than
a hell realm he thinks is paradise, so deluded is he in its vision of the
world. His every thought and action is governed by impulsivity and
contradictions of what Washington, Jefferson, Madison, and Lincoln
minted in their political scripture for America's democracy. So, what
psychiatrist or therapist or just any sane American citizen would
deny that he is a sociopathic or a fascist catalyst for an American
tragedy.

Chard deNiord

The Pigeon Parade

Fairy Tales were just the beginning: Hansel and Gretel taught
me about child abandonment, kidnapping, forcible detention,
cannibalism, and murder by cremation. Then I went to school
and learned The Pledge which didn't make much sense either.

I remember the words I heard: "*I led the Pigeons to the Flag
and to the Public for Richard Stans.*" I also learned to hide
under my desk when they dropped atomic bombs and not to
look at the flash and burn my eyes and have to wear glasses.

I learned the hard stuff after school about politics and power
about lies and betrayal about drinking beer and driving fast to
get girls but that only worked when I had a car and mine kept
getting smashed up. Hitchhiking on a date was not as romantic.

There was the business about poetry touching hearts and winning
favors but it had to be good poetry, not like this, and good poetry
was good, really good, and broke all the rules and created images
that were turned into symbols for things that didn't even really exist.

Poems with so much depending on a little red wheelbarrow could
jump start more hearts than a little red Mustang convertible. I tried
showing up for a date with a wheelbarrow once. She thought it was
cute, that was the word she used, *cute*, but didn't want to ride in it.

While I was playing with rhyme and free verse, creating new worlds
where hummingbirds and dragonfly wings powered constellations of
peace Presidents were using and abusing their powers in Viet Nam but
were finally beaten by protest marchers and those kids in black pajamas.

The latest authority is at it again, abusing power and creating a climate
of fear and oppression but the marchers are back too, rallying with banners
and cookies, and signs with slogans and phrases from the poetry of protest
reminding us about the Pied Piper, and not to simply follow the leader.

S. J. Cahill

My Broken Mirror

America, my broken mirror,
shards of dreams once so clear.
Each piece tells of the brave, the bold,
hopes and promises now ICE cold.

In the cracks, light whispers and hides
a slow dance of spirits each day into night.
In the jagged shard pieces, we still can see
our reflection shaped like a heart set free.

Though shattered, it beats, still shines bright,
resilient, my people still in the fight.
From the fallen fragments, we shall weave it again,
repair this broken mirror we still believe in.

With our hands, we will glue the glass,
We will mend the mind, we will heal the past.
In our new reflection, we'll make room for all to dance.
We'll give my broken mirror, my broken country, a second chance.

James Bird

I have never loved America more

never valued the American experiment
as I do today,
never felt the urgency of democracy as I now feel it.
Never tasted as now the mighty power
of "We, the People,"
a people derived
not from where you were born
but how you flocked to our shores and promises
and clung to Lady Liberty's ankles
as my people did before me.
I never saw how my life's delights
rest in the cradle of these first freedoms:
to believe, to worship, to speak, to read,
to gather, to protest, to insist,
all in safety
as my civic right and duty.
I never sensed that Lincoln's sacred call at Gettysburg
was a mandate for my time,
to ensure "that government
of the people, by the people, for the people,
shall not perish from the earth."
Now I love, and feel, and sense, and taste, and see.
America, I cry, come home.
Sins and all, America,
God shed his grace on thee.

Julie Berry
July 4, 2025

The Inheritance

Was it for this our fathers tried
To tread the English Channel tide
And fight the foe, and won, and died?

Normandy can't come again.
We can't produce that grade of man.

Who can remember sacrifice?
Who recalls how to pay the price?
What's sacrifice? What's shame? Such notions
Drowned in our domestic oceans.

The pear tree weeps its golden pendants,
Claiming the right of its independence.
The rabbits and the last-chance bees
Nibble and hum near the fragrant trees.

I hear the tree say, "Mercy, nurse."
A hymn, a threnody, a curse.
I stoop to smell the testament
Of what this tree has always meant.

"I give myself away, in truth
To generate a braver youth.
Eat up, and plant my timely seeds.
The world still gives what the human needs."

Gregory Maguire

The Bataan Death March

for Myrrl W. McBride
  who survived the Bataan Death March
   and for Gerald McBride

When the names were called out from
  The Bataan Death March,
    Tar and blood, the violent heat
      Scorched your forehead
        At the jungle's edge,
          The blue smoke of dead trees
            And the lilac smoke of corpses
              Seeped into you.

You were twenty years old
  When the winds came in
    Like flying glass
      Piercing your soul.

Who, coming out of torment,
  Hears the night's memory of hunger
    Closing the eyes of the dead?
      As your heart threw off its torque of tears,
        Scavenging for star anise
          and dorian seeds
            To sustain your friends
              Dying of starvation,
                Risking it all.

Take me to another place
  Of sacred tenderness
    Reaching for the abyss,
      Away from the destitution of time
        In the open.

Bring me home
  To the tents of music
    Where the crying never ends.

Terry Hauptman

This Goes on and On

those evaporated people's silhouettes etched
on Hiroshima's sidewalks, icons flash-
printed on the collective retina: *this
has been done, you and your kind are drawn
to do this. Bikini Atoll. Auschwitz.*

still watching the 2003 news, inside the gunsight
gaze: Bagdad's lights far below lurch toward
me, black and white, while a ghost shape, a plunging
bomb like a pale shark I'm tied to chases wandering
crosshairs into the speed-smeared city's night—
flares—lens-burst blind beyond white—already
normal—this sight—whether I want it
or not, whether I

knew I was

or not, I was, I am

branded—

the euphoric American broadcast voice: "Here's the luckiest
man in Bagdad!"—under the cartoon crosshairs, a tiny grey
bug of a car, driven surely by some clueless chipmunk, is creeping
out onto the long skinny bridge over the river—while the BIG
SURPRISE heads his way—*KAPOW!*—half the bridge
gone! the car stopped at the sudden brink—*imagine the size
of that little guy's eyes!*

down below, city blocks disintegrate in clouds of whirling particles
because I'm looking at them.

boats, one after another, bounding through waves coming toward me,
maybe carrying some kind of quick religion, some cruel heaven, vanish
in bursts of flames—scrolled glimpses, small

starvation trophies, my stomach aches and aches

John Steffler

**The Guadalupe
Camp Mystic
July 2025**

Sister June stood in the river,
dug her toes into the sandy bottom,
spread her arms from bank to bank,

stood there a long, long while.
The river   running clear   now. Gentle.

She leaned against the current,
shivered in the crisp night air.
Listened.

At last voices.

Campfire songs. The river had
heard them a million times. Loved them.
So too, Sister June.
Songs about bunnies and itsy-bitsy spiders
cockle shells and little bells
and Jesus.
Lots of songs about Jesus.

Jesus! Such a sweet and happy chorus!

The joy-filled notes rose from the water
then streaked down
Sister June's cheek and pooled
In the crease beside her lips.

She dabbed at it, dipped the tips of her
fingers into the water, felt its hunger.

The river will be blamed, for sure.
And yet, the river was just the river,
doing what rivers do
In its need to run to the sea.

As much as the river would be
blamed, so too, God,
and Sister June should know.

This was not her first Aftermath
after all.

They'll pray to God, and Jesus.
They'll send those prayers out
via satellite and landlines and
of course, from pulpits.
Of course.
Calls for mercy, calls for comfort,
calls for miracles.

But it isn't God, or Jesus,
who needs all those prayers,
now, is it?

God's received more prayers than hills have ants.
So many prayers.
Ancient, new. Sung spoken whispered.
Stacked in piles by the cat door, and crammed
beneath the sofa.

They'll drown out the tender notes,
riding on the stream, they'll be so
busy praying. It's a shame, because

what god loves is the same as the river:
the songs of little girls,
their wings as white as stars.

Kathi Appelt

You Think This is Hot?

"It's hotter than hell," you say. I wish it were.
I fear that hell will be much hotter, unless
this climate shift is just an early stir
of the pot we'll bubble in, divine finesse
consisting of the wherewithal to damn
ourselves without apocalyptic bother.
Say can you see the horns on Uncle Sam
as yet another zip-tied migrant father
strains helpless toward his confiscated child,
his Gaza sisters' babies maimed or starved,
or how both God and country are *sieg heiled*
in the MAGA Moloch that our voters carved
and kiss, a rich brat beast its white high priest?
"For inasmuch as you have done to the least . . ."

Garret Keizer

Raven's Protest Poem (from the film *Unseen*)

Who tore the pages from history's spine?
Who burned the last copy of dissent?
Who shuttered the libraries, declared books dangerous?
Who chained tongues with laws and leashes,
slapped warning labels on wisdom,
and outlawed curiosity like a crime against the Republic.

O teachers exiled to the shadows!
O librarians guarding the last embers of the Alexandria dream!
O poets whispering in underground cafés,
scratching manifestos into napkins,
O children locked in algorithmic loops,
trapped in the echo of their own reflections,
who will teach you to shatter the mirror,
to see beyond the frame?

I say: unchain the tongues,
unleash the books,
rip down the barricades of sanctioned thought!
I say: let knowledge crash like waves upon the desert,
flood the minds with forgotten voices,
drag history from the dungeons,
dust off the dangerous ideas and
read them aloud in the town square,
where every citizen, rich or ragged,
may drink freely from the fountain of truth—

Because when the books are burned, the people follow,
because when speech is silenced, silence becomes the master,
because a mind unfed is a mind enslaved,
because the only chains I will ever wear are
the words I did not speak.

Shalom Gorewitz

How to Offer Hope

Show up at the door
of the hopeless
with a tray of 2-inch terra cotta pots,
bright green shoots exhaling

possibility. Or,
fill a daffodil with a shot of
tequila and hum "Lovely Day"
by Bill Withers.

————

Jesus is out of town, so
the witches are representing
God, which in my opinion is just
as good, if not. Even.

*Jesus loves
the little witches,
all the little witches
of the world.*

————

Today I let holiness
hound me
as I push the light
away, falling into sleep

like a new favorite
cocktail. My aloneness
a new antidote
to loneliness.

———

If I sound like
I'm whining,
let me
rewrite this poem.

From here,
I cannot see anything
as less than everything
necessary.

Each stone in my shoe,
tangled line of communication,
loss of power resurrected
as April.

———

Let's Live Cam the river of our days, or
if we are young
and unemployed enough,
the river of our nights.

My home is under revision.
My home is a bridge
My home is a teenager.
My home

———

Horns, birds, sirens
zoom in the background.
You mute, and
the empty space leaves

watermarks of sounds,
circles
of motion
on my desk.

You are still here.
I still hear you
exhaling,
lucid with hope.

cin salach
July 2025

Aftermath Posturing

After the clip of the murder of a Black man jogging aired
on TV, now was the time
to take steep back
stairs to the sweltering peak attic, time to bring down . . .

those summer outfits stored in bins; and reeking
of plastic, to pop
the snapped container lids
and let them breathe. But once in the attic,

I never came down— the condition of weak,
overheated plastic, its toxic air.
I stumbled, crawled wounded-cowboy-like
to the fixed attic window for a view

from high up in a Best Western efficiency,
where, watching the tail end of a good cowboy film
sunset, shadows moved over
distant peaks or Western development?

Wherever I was, I couldn't lodge there,
but before I could flee, two Black businessmen—
they saw the clip, too— abruptly ended their stay
in my faux building, burst out my back door.

In my backyard, someday?
Their outfits already matched the season.
They had on light running suits
to make their flight home more comfortable.

Their suits were extraordinary: one, yellowish,
abstractly-designed; the other, a simple gray,
but it shimmered when the man inside moved,
so much so that I experienced a slippery sense

between the tips of my right thumb and index finger.
Summer wasn't coming. It had long been. *That sense:
wing powder!* I could be a boy again,
on my first day hunting butterflies, and so soon

fascinated by one landed on a flower,
its wings slowed. Hurt? Naw,
just exhausted. At rest, the wings
slowly working made it seem as if

it was catching its breath.
Or aping my winded heaves for oxygen,
after I gave it such a valiant chase. The bright-suited
businessman was my first butterfly, back then,

a Tiger Swallowtail—*Why would a tiger
swallow its tale?* Now, it was the evening
again, before dinner, when I raced up
to my bedroom to read, to find out more.

They didn't breathe
through a nose or mouth like mine.
Over time, a series of tiny holes
evolved along their abdomens, naturally.

Scott Withiam

I Am the Very Model of a Narcissistic Slanderer
(With apologies to W.S. Gilbert.)

I am the very model of a narcissistic slanderer.
The women like my style, I am a pretty slick philanderer.
I love my MAGA sycophants and all that far-right panderering.
And got myself elected through inventive gerrymandering.
I love to play the bully—got the whole world tariff-terrified
My whims are somewhat woolly but I spout them with a lot of pride.
I'm big on deportation, because immigrants aren't very nice!
That's why you should report them to the friendly folks who work at ICE.

My discourse is ingenious, I'm not handicapped by modesty.
No bogeys on my scorecard, I'm not handicapped by honesty.
I know the Hitler playbook and I follow it the best I can.
Democracy is dead—it does not figure in my master plan.
Autocracy—now there's the thing!—appeals more to my vanity.
I'll shut the country down, then put the kibosh on your liberty.
My National Guard will stamp down civil protest with their baseball bats
And round up all reactionary WOKE and sniveling Democrats.

I've got Fox News on side supporting all my crackpot fantasies.
I've loaded the Supreme Court, now they do exactly as I please.
I've started in on women's rights—whoever thought they needed 'em?
And as for gender-benders—it's high time we superseded 'em
With virile men and buxom girls, we'll make this country straight again.
There'll be no more elections, I will simply do away with them.
I'll elevate my favorite goons by making them all generals
We'll conquer Canada and steal its water, gas and minerals.
Oh, I am the very model of a tyrant with a powerful grudge.
The only court you'll get me in's the one where I sit as the judge.

Tim Wynne-Jones

Fall:
It's the Beginning of the End…

The Dry Bones

"My river is mine own, and I have made it for myself."
—Book of Ezekiel 29:3

And into the heavens, as on a bright day after rain,
there came the shapes of four creatures,
and they each had the likeness of a man,
and each man had four wings outstretched
and each wing had four eyes emblazoned, wide open,
given to weeping at the worlds they contained:

an eye-world of light, of fire and air,
of water and its mirror, heart and its first fear;
and in each world were four names,
entangled in its forest of letters,
whereupon I could read: Dow Jones, Cargill,
Chevron, and DeKalb of the frozen seed,
bearing but once and giving up its need;

and under each name were discovered four meanings,
literal, figurative, rational, dim,
and under each meaning a counter-meaning,
with its likeness of Freud, Marx, Hegel, and Lacan;
and the four figures passed as one overhead,
their wingtips linked like molten silver joined.

For I, Ezekiel, had been given to eat
the very substance of God,
and my eyes were open and my mouth spoke,
as spring opens winter and winter closes fall;
and the earth turned rightly, to my senses sweet.
Son of man, they called me, a proverb and a sign.

Say: I am a sign of the city, the cauldron
where men burn down to desire.
Say: I am the proverb of nothing and one,
boiling over the fire, rising out of belief
and falling, like a tyrant, out of derision alone.

And lo, a likeness, as of the appearance of fire,
the error of presence, of nothing as one,
and lo, another likeness, the appearance of water,
the error of absence, of something as none;
for water surrounds all shapes that enter
but has no shape of its own,
and fire is the shape of ruin alone.

For the princes of the sea
shall cast their garments upon Land's End:
their scholar's robes, sharkskin suits,
and alligator shoes, their Nikes,
Reboks, and Chuvashian mittens
knitted by the children of shepherds,
by tinsmiths and ladies' men,
in the dark at the back of the store;
for the princes of fire consume what they love,
with the reckless ambition of gods.

Yea, as I spoke to dry bones that lay upon the earth,
they danced into being, and chattered, one and one,
down the hallways of my desert, the thresholds of my river.
For the Lord builds ruined palaces and plants desolation,
he receives what is absent; possesses all that is gone.

(Ezekiel)

Paul Hoover

Palimpsest

Even medieval monks knew erasure
left a mark, vellum could not be scraped new,
the past was always there
beneath the latest script.

When a rose paradise is paved,
defense renamed war, and masked men
descend with impunity on anyone with non-white skin,
even if we cannot protest in person
because we are ill, because we are caring
for someone who needs us, young or old or in-between,
we can speak the palimpsest of our time,
starting small and building—
       the Gulf of Mexico,
       vaccines save lives
       all humans are created equal,
       all humans have the same rights
            to life, liberty, love, and respect,
            to pursue their happiness in safety and security.

We can remember the truth,
speak it aloud when we wake in the night,
unable to return to sleep for the noise of the latest scraping.

Katherine Quimby

Labor Day

ripple-hills hint
a range of Spring-deluged
dull yellows rusty corals

oil-rich kingpins
poke the planet
change climate air & sea

labor protests oligarch thieves
federal troop-threat
conjures: Hay Market riot
coal-miners' union-bust

throngs of unsheltered workers
rent spikes feed greed
tents banned prisons thrive

geese gaggles flee
rivers too shallow for reeds
dead trout won't rise up

Elisabeth Fred

The Candidates Debate

Moderator: What is the sound of a thousand angry people in the streets?
Candidate 1: Sadness and pragmatism.
Candidate 2: Is it lunch already?

Moderator: A child walks into the room and sits next to you. What do you say?
Candidate 1: Wash your hands. Listen to your mother. I'm not your father.
Candidate 2: I'm glad you found work.

Moderator: Do you have a message for the country?
Candidate 1: Smoke, don't smoke—you'll live.
Candidate 2: You're worse off but think of all you've learned

Moderator: What are your qualifications?
Candidate 1: I have lived by habit and what doesn't hurt.
Candidate 2: Genius, Xanax.

Moderator: Any parting words?
Candidate 1: You're only as good as you dare to be bad.
Candidate 2: I'm not here to entertain. I'm here to sell hot dogs.

Mike Puican

Election

a country holds its place
by every screen
in every room in every chair
afraid to look up afraid
                                 to look away

on edge on the edge of the seat
tuned to the same
breaking news broken
by the next breaking
                            news breaking news

when the moment happens
to end this heartless reign
what will you then be holding
gun or pen
                  whiskey or champagne

Wyatt Townley

It's the Beginning of the End and I'm Here to Tell You

what it feels like to know
and to not be believed.
      Conspiracy theory
they say. Toss out
      crazy
      overreacting
      ignorant as the other side.
But the site of my knowing
comes from the woke side
      (re: empathy)
comes from the heart-side,
and the logic side, too
even with no facts or evidence
but what poet
ever gave you evidence of the moon's
yearning stare that was a cold hard fact
and not a buried bone
unearthed from their own
unknowing body?

I can tell you how alone inside my own skin
I feel for knowing what I know—
what I wish I didn't know—
what I see in our future
which was a future my Jewish ancestors
could never know.
But I do
because someone with my blood
in a German town,
or a Hungarian one, depending on the side
      (re: how many sides to a [insert one]
      family/poem/moon/democracy/aisle/border?)
had the sense, or luck, or privilege to flee
so they could whisper down to me,

in, or through, my bones. A voice
coming from the other side
of the veil this time
to tell me what this world
will become.

Samantha Kolber

The Right Tyrant

I.

Blue mantle of the Madonna: ultramarine,
powdered lapis lazuli from the caves of Afghanistan,
pigment used by Michelangelo to paint his angels.
Next, the chemist in his lab, deepening the carmine
made with blood from the female cochineal,
but surprised by red gone to purple gone to blue
when poured over animal blood, that pigment named
Prussian Blue, used by Van Gogh in his starry night,
Hokusai in his blue wave, and used, too, to dye
the uniforms of soldiers lying bloodied and dead
on the fields at Waterloo. Later, another chemist
in another lab who, stirring the blue with a dirty spoon,
finds cyanide hiding there, calls it Zyklon—"cyclone"—
the poison waiting for more chemists and more labs
and more wars and for the right tyrant to come along.
Soon enough, one comes, and so comes Zyklon-B.,
pushed through the pipes and the showers heads
of Auschwitz, dyeing the chamber bricks blue.

II.

"It was ever thus," they say: the right tyrants always
come along - trembling little egos, fragile, brutal, looking
for cyclones of their own. "Cold mothers," says Freud.
"Toxic fathers," says Dr. Phil. "I miss my parents,"
says Napoleon, as does our own Strongman, a sound-byter,
Mommy's demented Donny Boy, Daddy's junior version,
a con man coached by Roy Cohn in the Art of The Lie,
pushing for the next genocide, *Mein Kampf* on the nightstand,
he's tweeting love letters to dictators, sending asylum-seekers
to Sudan, building border fences to keep out the people
poisoning his white blood. See him mock and taunt, turn

his head away from the graves of losers on the beaches
of Normandy, dream of gold hotels built on top of the bodies
of dead Gazans, hear him praise ICE-men in black masks
yanking people from their cars, watch him pass out duct tape
to keep us from speaking, to silence the jesters, see him hold his
borrowed Bible upside-down, loving Christ to pieces, loving
Democracy to shreds, hugging the Red White & Old Glory Blue
field of stars, grabbing pussies, cockadoodling his hot daughter,
telling the press to shut up, telling journalists to drop dead,
boasting out loud I'm a genius, smarter than all my generals,
strong as a bull, when I came down that escalator with my red tie
pointing at my penis, I came swollen, big, beautiful and anointed,
you better know I'm the right one, and I've stopped so many wars,
I know all the right words and I god damn deserve that fucking Prize.

Julie Larios

Trump, a Philippic

His "mind-forged manacles" are clanging in
the streets of America. Listen
if you can. They clang but never rhyme as they drag
behind Ugolino* who's risen again
somehow from Circle 9 in Hell, where Dante
thought he'd stay for good, but no. He's here again
with a runway do for devils to land on
and then deplane inside his head; forget his heart
whose fragile wire never reached his head
and dangles still in his chest, unhitched
and dead.

*Count Ugolino is a historical figure who, with his sons and grandsons, was imprisoned and starved to death in Pisa in 1288. Dante Alighieri immortalized him in Canto XXXIII of the *Inferno* as a traitor condemned to the Ninth Circle of Hell, where he gnaws on the skull of his enemy, Archbishop Ruggieri, who betrayed him. The specific details of his story, including whether he resorted to cannibalism, are left deliberately ambiguous by Dante, though he is clearly depicted in Hell for his betrayal.

Chard deNiord

american dog

    thumps on the door. odious i.c.e.-guys who repose
with guns outside a small house. a boy answers weakly . . .
the i.c.e.-dog sniffs for citizens, then sends in a distant,
but sympathetic look: *i would not kill you, but i might*
drag you to the ground if he says the word. now, I must
nose through your house. your shocked mother. your bricklayer
father. they are bones standing up.
    the boy says, *we've come to call this love.*
    i don't know how I got this awful job. i woke up hypnotized.
men in masks with opaque eyes. the masks say hate what I am.
inside the caves of each skull, a beast in a crib.
    the boy asks, *am I to be lost or found?*
    lost. past your crayon house. past the black line of the river.
    but the world is everywhere, says the boy.
    dog says, *this is no longer the world. this is a place*
of many secrets.
    I have friends. I have whatever I had.
    your soul is a blameless flower. mine's been replaced with a red
and blue fire.

Chris Solís Green

The Edge of the Gorge

"Man is by nature a political animal." —Aristotle

Canyons between us we can't understand.
Tell me stranger at this political divide,
what thresholds you failed to cross,

what you lost, that there's more
than nothing between us.

Freedom of thought, soft as Lambs-ear,
cashmere, fragrant as thyme-walked
ground. Somewhere between love & hate,

atheist & saint. Even Tolstoy wrote first of war.
Peace falls like spring rain, an eagle feather.

Tell me neighbor of thresholds you failed
to cross, what you lost, that there's more
than nothing between us.

"Can you divide this apple into three halves?"
your daughter asked, feeding other hungry mouths

as she opened hers. Division as portioning.
Peace drops like a whisper between prairie warbler
and lark bunting, one feeder, tern and gull, one shore,

low tide and high. Over mountains, plains, drop
all your thoughts, friend, until edges give way, tell me
of thresholds you failed to cross, what you lost,

that there's more than nothing between us. I'm wary
watching the broad-winged hawk circle, dive & rise.

Let stones shake from the ground up.
I want to feel the lift of your breath
on my cheek as you speak.

Judith Janoo

The Watchlist

These motherfuckers put my professor
on a watchlist.
She is an eruption of knowledge, passion,
and political understanding, but
they can't have a powerhouse like that running around,
opening the eyes of the next generation to
the patterns of fucked-uppery imbedded in the workings of the world.
She has lit a fire under me, as have others,
to write, to speak, to read, to act, to protest–
like my life depends on it.
She is brilliant,
dispelling intelligence with humor and grace and
kindness and understanding.
She is breath-taking and breath-giving,
as she feeds our minds, our hearts, our souls, and
is fed by the feeding.
She is Jewish, like me, but has been
flagged by the listmakers for anti-semitism because
she is not a Zionist.
She has been on the watchlist list for nine years,
she tells us, and she's honest about what's going on–
the dozens of death threats, and
plenty of other kinds made on her body,
her hard work, her freedom of speech,
her career.
No uniform sought to protect her then,
but now that some white man
killed the other white man that put her on the
watchlist, and some hard-core right-wing nationalists
are thirsting for the lives of all those crucial educators,
—*now*, the school suggests police stationed
in classrooms,
their bullet-proof vests protecting their bodies,
rather than hers, or ours.

To this institution, we are nothing more than a room full
of liabilities, a lawsuit waiting to happen
if God forbid a student caught a bullet,
a brick, or a baton,
that was meant for her.
I listen as the single black student in our class
recounts their experience from three weeks ago
of a racially motivated hate-crime.
I picture a cop in the door frame and
I see the words of my peers—
—the students of color,
the queer ones, the Muslims,
the Jews
—I see the scrolls of deeply-thought and nurtured meaning unravel
off their tongues like scripture.
The officer steps in, past his looming door frame,
trampling those magnificent scrolls of buzzing protest,
holy anti-capitalism, critical race theory,
anti-colonialism,
aspirations of equality, of lifting up—
but all he lifts up are those well-learned papers,
pulsing with potential, ready to burst into action,
just to crumple them, shred them, and
shove them back down the throats
from which they came.

Alyx Young

White House Peace Vigil

*(William Thomas was the first guardian of the Peace Vigil.
Forty-four years later, Phillipos, Thomas's godson, may be the last.)*

"Can you Livestream?" my friend Nadine asks.
She's holding a giant plastic bag, jammed with signs,
as she calls Phillipos, the Vigil's Guardian.
"People need to know what's happening."

This is the third time they've come for the vigil.
What will they take this time?

"Get rid of it!" President Trump said two weeks ago.
Friends and volunteers raced to the vigil that night.
We hugged each other in relief.
"It's still here!"
A local musician played guitar and crooned his new song,
"Trump is a Punk-Ass Bitch"
by the light the 88-foot American flagpole,
posted in the north lawn of the White House.

Now, I realize I don't have any photos of the vigil.
I've taken this odd blue tarp structure for granted.
Its hodgepodge of signs on wooden stands,
clipped to the tarp, and spread across the bricks,
about Palestine, Nuclear weapons, Iran,
Guantanamo, Iraq, Tibet, Afghanistan,
Ukraine, Kashmir, Trump, Free Speech,
all part of the White House scene for me.
I don't agree with every single sign,
but I'll always believe they have a right to be here.

I also thought Phillipos would always be
sitting here in his wheelchair,
his long dreads wrapped in a colorful t-shirt,

Palestinian flag flying by his side.
That's how things had been for the last seven months
I had been protesting at the White House.

*　*　*

We call it, "The People's House"
because it's paid for with our tax dollars.
The Peace Vigil is the spot,
for the people to protest.
Since June 1981,
people have been protesting for peace
and against nuclear armament,
and so much more.

Someone must be at the Peace Vigil at all times,
24 hours a day,
every day of the year,
in rain, sleet, snow, wind or DC's excessive humid heat.
They must be awake.
No sleeping at the Peace Vigil.

Phillipos is there so often he's like a permanent
human monument. But from 4:30-7:30 a.m.
on weekdays, Craig watches over it.
"I met William Thomas years ago,"
he tells me one night when I stayed at the vigil.
"I was walking around the White House and sat with him.
He told me his values and why he was here.
They were my values.
I stayed."

At 7:30 a.m. on weekdays, Neil arrives.
Like Craig, he's been doing this shift for over a decade.
Weekends are often just Phillipos.
who has done "a lot of 72-hour shifts."

                              ***

Park Police won't take the tarp from over Phillipos' head,
so they come on a Sunday, at 6:55 a.m.,
just after he wheels away for a bathroom break.

At 24, Will is the youngest of the volunteers.
He came to DC from Michigan for 90 days,
to protest fascism.
He protested all day at the White House,
then camped in the woods of DC at night.
He made friends, found a family.
When Park Police came for the vigil,
he leapt on the tarp,
not caring that they'd arrest him.
He had come to protect peace and democracy.
They left everything but the tarp,
that time, only detained Will for 10 minutes.

Lindsay, from rural upstate New York,
watched Trump's press conference.
She had never been to the Peace Vigil
but the message of peace resonated.
"I'm driving to DC to protect it," she told her husband.
"Get a good night's sleep," he said, "then drive there."

She was grateful for the sleep,
as she held her homemade peace sign,
made of metal and twine,
all Sunday,
at the tarp-less vigil,
a red beach umbrella
sheltering its guardians now.

That night we celebrated the vigil's survival.
People poured through the White House plaza,
bringing food and conversation.

So many people connected to the vigil,
volunteers from years ago stopped by.

A Ukrainian protester and his fifteen-year-old daughter,
decked out in a traditional embroidered dress,
told tales of driving across the country in their trailer,
educating people about the Ukrainian-Russian war.

* * *

The second time, they took the large wooden signs,
that said, "Anti-Nuclear, Peace Vigil, Since 1981,"
and the beach umbrella,
at dawn, again.
When only Will was there, again.
He tried to stop them, again.
Handcuffed, again,
Let go, again.

This time, the third time,
they come at dusk, not dawn.
Nadine, Amy and I are watching over.
Nadine knows what is happening.
"Grab as much as you can," she says,
before the Park Police have even approached.

"Parks Closed!" the officer calls.
"Everyone needs to leave!"

Nadine learned about the Peace Vigil in 2018.
She was at the White House protesting for Black Lives Matter.
When a fence was erected at the White House,
protesters turned it into the Black Lives Matter fence.
Nadine became its guardian.
The BLM fence was removed.
BLM Plaza was dismantled by Trump,
but Nadine still watches over the Peace Vigil.

After the tarp was gone,
Nadine sealed all their cardboard signs,
with clear contact paper,
to protect them from the elements.

All three of us hobble towards H street,
carrying as many signs as we can.
Amy's brought the vigil's funds & papers.
No one is able to bring the chairs or speakers.
Park Police ask for Nadine's ID, tell her
she can pick up the speakers and chairs,
later at a warehouse.

I'm Livestreaming for my first time ever,
telling my meager followers about the vigil.
Someone yells from nearby.
"You're tearing down history!"
It's Will.
Phillipos has arrived, too.
I interview Phillipos for the Livestream.
"I'm contacting the ACLU," he says.

Park Police take down the yellow tape.
They act like this is just a regular park closing,
the kind that happens daily.
Phillipos and Nadine leave to put the signs in his car.
I rush forward to check out what's left.
Will follows behind.

There's nothing,
just brick and grass.

I sit there on the curb that separates
brick from the grass, holding my personal protest sign.
It's large and says, "Protect Free Speech,
Not Trump's Fragile Ego" with a cartoon drawing,

Trump covering money bags with his tiny orange hands.
In a speech bubble he says, "Jimmy Kimmel was mean to me."

"Can you take my picture, Will?"
I hand him my phone.
He takes the photo of me at the barren site.

Phillipos and Nadine join us.
Someone else takes a photo of all of us.
Soon a Washington Post reporter and photographer come.
They'll tell our story.
Will and I leave around 11 pm.
Nadine and Phillipos guard the vigil spot
all night.

Phillipos returns the next day,
and the next,
and the next.
Others join him.

We are the vigil now.
We will endure.

The Peace Vigil is still the spot
for people to protest for peace.

"We call it The People's House,
because it's paid for with our tax dollars,"
I call out to the tourists on H Street,
as they search for the White House,
past the yellow police tape,
in the twilight dimming Lafayette Park.

Robin Galbraith

The climb

The man on the bus does not believe in evolution.
He argues that if it were true, we'd see the dead
ends, the broken bits. We'd have bones and footprints,
remnants of what tried and failed. I argue the changes
were slight, and happened over time. That they either
dissolved into the present—the surviving—or they
ended their reign as they were on the day they died.
It's simple: adapt or die. But which one will we be?

I wish that all the creatures had the time to lift their faces
to the sky as they hunted and gathered or grazed, as they
gasped and gnawed and dragged themselves out of the den,
out of the dark, out of this dry and depleted world like a
hope that drives forever forward despite the odds. This is
why we must remember the walruses on that island packed
so tightly together that they cannot touch the rocky earth.
Whiskered and bleating, they bleed. Fluffed and puppy-faced.
They all seek a space to rest their bodies. Some turn away
from the crush of the crowd and climb the rocks. Above the
frigid waters, their enormous bodies flopping as they strive
ever upward towards the light, towards the open, where
they finally close their eyes, lift their faces to the breeze.

January 6: I pick up my dad's ashes from the funeral home
as an insurrection scales the Capitol. I am struck by how the
ordinary—the fabrics, the faces—are made strange by the climb.
Not unlike the walruses, who, when they finally feel hunger,
open their watery dog eyes and, with a trust they've known
since the age of the ice, throw themselves to the air.

Katie Moritz

The Elephant in the Room

"Living next to you is in some ways like sleeping with an elephant."
—Canadian Prime Minister Pierre Elliot Trudeau
on US/Canada relations, March 25, 1969

The Elephant has insomnia
and indigestion.

He rolls over and
the bed heaves.
My head hits the ceiling.

He grunts, twists.
My toes scramble for purchase.

"Can I get you anything, dear?"

His feet kick. His toenails slice my ankles.
A whimper escapes me.

"Some tea, maybe?"

He farts percussively
and the smell gallops, ricocheting off the walls.

"Camomile, perhaps?"

A belch explodes from places I don't want to think about.

Cautiously, small mice tiptoe
between the stiff hairs of his tough hide,
across to my side of the bed.
Quietly, we share cheese and digestive biscuits.

A roar blasts our crumbs.
His trunk flails and crashes
        smashes his bedside lamp.
And his side of the room is in darkness.

The mice and I huddle under my lamp,
Cling to our raft,
Tell each other stories
        of friendship and love.
We sing songs 'round campfires
And stay awake, vigilant,
Waiting for daylight.

Amanda West Lewis

What the Alt National Park Service Taught Me

We teeter the edge of catastrophe all is not well sisters I will show you
what I learned lying under the trees listening as old women wont to
do I cannot keep my mouth shut cannot keep my pen still   poetry
has always been the perfect site for resistance to measure in breaths
last lost stanzas of freedom silence is compliance I keep on versing &
versing in secret alphabets my body crowding with thorns I've bled on
the matters worked incomprehensible by overreliance on metaphor
& allegory they can't take the wilderness out of the old girl—resist—
spring light might sing different stars might twinkle logic not just
for scholars may I remind you—resist—I know I'm posting too much
about the political situation but seems irresponsible to get back to
you in mythological doodads & paper swords I keep on versing &
versing—resist—the time is dire Once I placed my hands on a oak to
feel the tree purr into my palms emerged from between trees moss in
my hair dirt beneath my nails sung another aggressive abracadabra
testament to what can be built from acorns & twigs here is a flesh
flower to fill your heart hole with love to fill vacancy a poem written
to the tune of no regrets my breath tastes of fire & nicotine—resist—
move forward like you'd move through a haunted forest with great
care & honed night vision give aid to the creatures in need I will
remind you again about resilience resistance responsibility move
quiet as the witch who just stopped her chanting & settled in to drink
the spirits of her vanquished enemies—resist—

Susen James

Destination Despair

Writing poetry is difficult, especially when being asked
to reach into the core and draw down, or up, if you like,
emotions that may be private and painful, feelings that
are best left alone, stones unturned, that once exposed
could well be lifted up and thrown, weaponizing them.

What is it about our nature that sends us poking down
and looking around for stories that we once had buried
or repressed, sealed away in the darkest forbidden places
hidden in a Christ-like cave with a boulder rolled in front
to keep truth buried so it would not wake us in the night.

But we all know how that turned out—the Houdini thing
a great escape or someone set him free so now and forever
he reminds us to be good and generous and kind and help
our neighbors build an ark if and when the skies grow dark
and the rains return and the waters rise and we despair.

No one really knows where he went or what he did when
he left the cave but I for one wish he'd go up and chat
with his father, you know, have a good heart to heart talk
with the old man and tell him it's time for a miracle or two.
Tell him to straighten out the war business and the climate
and then, and then, while he's at it, straighten out politics
because I swear to God, politics today fill me with despair.

S. J. Cahill

Final Exam

I dreamed I was in Washington, DC
I didn't know what I was doing there or why
anyone would want to be there, especially,
with a towering pointing finger national monument,
while my own finger traveled down a thick document's table of contents
    listing people,
no, people's most feared dreams, till it stopped on *Dream of Missing*
and so failing a Final Exam. Beneath that heading read *Causes*
extreme panic and dread, which is fueled by the projection that failing leads

to the loss of an opportunity to secure a better future.
For myself or for others?
As for myself, I went to my five-star hotel room to change
for someone else's dinner. I needed dress shoes.
I only had the very worn running sneakers I wore. I did have the good sense
to bring along a fresh change of clothes. Despite worn sneakers,
I could look my very best on top. Anyone could. After changing,

though, what else could I do
but put the same feet right back into the same worn sneakers and run out
and jump into a wood-paneled elevator with intricately gilded plasterwork
protruding and collecting a lot of dust. The elevator doors closed.
And then, opened again on the same floor. *Why does this always happen*
when most people are in a hurry to get someplace important? I asked myself.

Nobody was there.
No, there *was* someone there.
I just wouldn't hear them.
On stepped a bleached blonde bouffant in a swishing long black gown
trailing beneath a knee-length fur coat.
Its partner or date— a large tux— used the bouffant as a shield,
as if that was enough to slink by unnoticed. Hardly. The tux
faced the back corner of the elevator like a bat

in a gilt cave going down. The bouffant fixed on my beat-up sneakers.
"My tux used to run on a track!" it said.
"And soon he'll be putting in his miles again,
but tonight, will be *the* last exam."
Since it was Washington, I tried to understand the bouffant

as making a declaration: no more final exams. Slight progress, at least,
on the national front: no more tests to miss, so no more bad dreams,
so no more anxiety, a few less feelings of *I'll never get ahead*.

"Brilliant," I shouted.   The bat/tux hunched forward.
Was it my suggestion of light? "Here's what's brilliant,"
the blonde bouffant said. "The present administration
has called our evening dinner with the outgoing president
the president's last exam, so the populace continues to think
the president receives full medical exams, when
he never did." "Wait a minute," I said, "your large tux is . . ."

"That's right," the bouffant said, "Physician to the President,
and tonight, the only thing my tux has to attend to is an intimate goodbye
   dinner
with the president." The tux bent as if sick. *Was that what the election was
from the start,* I thought, a*n intimate goodbye dinner?*
when the elevator lurched to a halt. I never felt us going down.

The elevator doors opened two feet below the lobby floor.
We had to help each other out. Together,
the bouffant and tux couldn't pull me out. I climbed out myself.
Once in the lobby, the bouffant noted the weather outside.
The Washington winter had already changed to a cold rain.

"It's just impossible to prepare for the weather here," the bouffant said.
The tux's collar turned up and the top button of the bouffant's fur secured.
By the time you two reach the White House, I said,
that fur will be soaked slick as a runt kitten I once rescued.

The bouffant and tux stepped back,
as if to say, *This is how you say goodbye to us?*

I explained. Tippy, a former dog of mine,
had been an aging male shepherd mix on his last leg,
my reason for adopting the kitten I'd named Monitor.
Sprawled under the dining room table, Tippy often pinned Monitor
under a paw, and licked and licked and licked,
as if its mother, to keep Monitor clean.
It left Monitor's fur totally slicked and nasty.

"This is ridiculous. Let's go," the bouffant demanded.
"No," the tux said— the bat finally spoke!—
"this raises an interesting election question, one I long entertained,
and lately, have posed again: Why is it
that every time one breed crosses the line
to take care of another breed,
like they'd take care of their own,
people get so excited?"

I was about to tell the Tux
Tippy's licking didn't last,
but before I could,
they were in the revolving doors
and launched into a soaking rain.

Scott Withiam

Have You Ever Met a Nefarian?

Whenever crops wither, or taxes rise steep,
Or your pillow goes missing when you need sleep,
Don't question the weather, the markets, or fate—
It's the Perpetual Nefarians, the people we hate.

If your cat claws the curtains, if soup tastes like glue,
If your socks lose their partners (they always do),
Don't bother with reason, don't bother to sleuth,
It's obvious the Nefarians stole the truth.

The bridge has collapsed? The mayor looks grim?
The milk went all sour? The lights have gone dim?
The Nefarians plotted, they cackled, they schemed—
Their mission is wrecking whatever you dreamed.

They fiddle with traffic, they tangle the cables,
They bring chaos to offices, mislabel labels.
When whispers spread shadows, fear, and mistrust,
The Nefarians clearly are messing with us.

So blame them for thunder, for crime, for drought,
For the words that you meant but forgot to shout.
The world would be perfect, both sunny and fair,
If only the Perpetual Nefarians weren't everywhere.

Shalom Gorewitz

October 2025

The famous poet who lives in Athens
    reads her poem, "Ostracon,"
written the day after the election.

I wish she brought a suitcase
    of broken pottery so we could
exile this entire administration

but are not enough shards
    to name everyone who voted
for this. Medicaid cuts affect millions

of disabled people, including my daughter.
    ICE agents raid Canal Street,
Apartment buildings and zip-tie children

still warm from their beds. Vultures
    circle overhead and hide
their faces in the trees. In the birthplace

of democracy, the Parthenon is free
    from scaffolding for the first time
in 200 years. Here, the East Wing

of the White House has been demolished
    to build a ballroom, a bunker.
They shut down the government and SNAP

is suspended. They know when people
    are hungry, anger will follow.
The pottery is rough and cold in my hands.

Jennifer Franklin

Homenaje a los silbatos

Y lo digo así en plural
Honremos a los silbatos
Que ya se oyen por la Clark
Justo en Tacos Hernández
Que resoplen vatas y vatos
Que pararon a Matías
En la vuelta de la esquina

Honremos a los silbatos
Son negros y de metal
Amarillos y de plástico
Y nos libran de todo mal

Quién imaginó un día
Amar tanto a los silbatos
Avisan que hay embozados
Mas no los oyó Matías

Dicen los rapid responders
Silbato de sonido roto
Si Bovino anda en el área
Silbato de sonido largo
Porque arrestan a Matías

Ah, los silbatos
Que son como el ticolote
Y el canto del cardenal
Que previenen del peligro
A gente como Matías

Ahí vienen los federales
Vestidos de mercenarios
O acaso son mercenarios
Vestidos de federales

Son Bovinos embozados
¡Activemos los silbatos!
Que se oigan en Rogers Park
Que retumbe San Jerónimo
Que se llevan a Matías
Que es mi rumait y mi amigo
Whistle!
Whistle!
Whistle!

Raúl Dorantes

Homage to the Whistles

And that's how I say it, in the plural
Let's honor the whistles
Heard now on Clark Street
Right by Tacos Hernández
Let everyone keep blowing them
Because they've stopped Matías
Just around the corner

Let's honor the whistles
They are black and made of metal
Yellow and made of plastic
And they deliver us from evil

Who could imagine a day
Of so much love for whistles
They warn of masked men
But Matías didn't hear them

The rapid responders say
A short whistle
If Bovino's in the area
A long whistle
Because they're arresting Matías

Ah, the whistles
Are like the owl
And the song of the cardinal
Keeping people like Matías
Out of danger

Here come the federal agents
Dressed like mercenaries
Or maybe they're mercenaries
Dressed like federal agents

They're Bovinos in masks
Activate the whistles!
Let them be heard in Rogers Park
Let them resound at St. Jerome's
Because they're taking Matías
My roommate and my friend
          Whistle!
                    Whistle!
                              Whistle!

Raúl Dorantes (translated by Mary Hawley)

First Tipping Point, October 13, 2025

Today, Earth reached its first irreversible tipping point,
coral reef collapse. Were you paying attention?
Off-balance visions take over our televisions,
an auditorium filled with heavy military

medals worn by unsmiling generals, admirals,
tips away from a painted clown, his low-browed
marionette onstage, their rambling war-fighting
blather fouling the air. Men and women hold their noses,

onscreen and off. A continent away, imbalance on the street,
Portland Frog's stare-down out-weighs a masked gang,
military wannabees. Too dear to us, social media
fascinates while our political and natural worlds fall apart

before our very eyes. Coral reefs bleach and die,
evict their fishy residents, consign them to slow
death, to forgetting. Earth's balance falters, leans
toward the sun, melts ice sheets—second tipping point—

destroys rainforest—third. Burning deserts expand,
wind-blown they creep   grain   by   grain.
                    Earth's frail balance

                                        tips over.

                    Do you not hear that hot desert wind howl?
                    Does it not blast heat into your already parched mouth?

                         Will it choke your children?
                         How will they die? How will you?

                    Do you even know what you are willing to die for,
                         fight for? Wasn't Earth enough?

What about that lone brilliant cloud sailing   across our last
    blue-blue   autumn   sky?

Sharon Darrow

Forest

We're subjects of the wind, you may have heard.
We grow together, speak and moan and sing.
We harmonize our branches for a bird
to nest or roost, the mating birds of spring.
We like sun's rays, we like a raindrop's ping.
We grow a leaf to make delicious air.
When lightning breaks, we feel the suffering.
We are this paper and this house. We care
for you and try to make you more aware.
We read your books and write a tremulous
inscription on a sky no longer bare:
to cloud to grave to field to sea to us.
We listen closely, standing by in trust,
then razed by chainsaws and a glutton's lust.

Mary Meriam

Mud Covenant

Empty of argument and praise of trees,
I only sit with cats nearby, a fool
miscalculating loss and gain of bees.
I tried to be your mother, but my rule
has only been ignored, and now the cool
of gifts of breath, of polar bears and air
melt swiftly into hell, the wretched drool
of death till Earth has nothing left to wear.
The wind you hear in forests won't be there.
To scorch a planet to a ball of flames,
the sun will rise, a bully with a stare.
I see your citizens of greedy games,
stabbing my flesh with drills and sucking blood.
You will not conquer me. You will be mud.

Mary Meriam

Colossus

Let rip the terrified and tiny cat
with tail and jaw, with pouncing leap and bite,
her sultry black thick fur with dabs of white,
let tell, let at, direct her towards the rat
before the population turns expat,
the jets jam-packed in never-ending flight.
One feline-witchy wonder-wander night,
we see her claws, we see her pointed hat,
one flick and in her teeth, the universe
of wickedness becomes a tasty treat.
She saves some sins for later in her purse,
and rescues us. She has enough to eat
of crunchy hate for breakfast, juicy curse,
the evil of the liar and the cheat.

Mary Meriam

I Mostly Ignore the Horrors

If my teeth didn't exist, I'd be grinding my gums down to dust,
pulverizing bone. This coffee I drink needs to be microwaved.
The kids need to be picked up from school, brought to the health

center for their Covid shots. Halloween litters the hardwood.
I need to vacuum before the dog inhales the wrappers. I've been up
too early, teaching too long, my face spasms. I wonder what's
    trapped in there.

I mostly ignore the horrors. I have to. My family needs me. Maybe
it's not a coincidence that in 2025 I had to change
up my medication, add a new one, the same antipsychotic

my mother is on. Genetics are powerful, but politics
are more so, and perhaps the two are linked somehow. It's difficult
to tell where the clench comes from. My eyes sag. Inside my mouth

everything is tight. My skull has holes where it shouldn't.
The doodle curls like a conch in my lap. It is only with her warmth
that I can relax the rigidity of my jaw. The month of January

I cried every day, and by July I was agoraphobic. The horrors
continue, but the algorithm sends reels of doodles and plants,
my curation successful, and still the world

is collapsing around us, the trees weeping, and my pandemic baby
has turned five; rides a pony around a ring, her smile
bigger than the contusions we all feel,

the treatment taken away from us. Everyone is happy
until the balloons begin to pop. There is no safety in this world,
but was there ever?

Adrienne Gruber

A Delicate Balance

WE REGRET TO INFORM YOU...

Your account is overdue.
The leak we inspected means you need a new roof.
Your policy doesn't include the coverage you requested.
The office you are trying to reach is no longer in existence.
Your loan application is rejected due to a weak credit score.

STILL, I AM PLEASED TO NOTE...

The Autumn sun feels like someone's crazy for my old skin.
Four singing frogs hold regular concerts in my backyard.
My grandson sent me a photo of the Northern Lights.
I dreamt my granddaughter swallowed a butterfly.
I'm learning to play the flute.

Louise Hawes

Riding on a Cloud

Riding on a cloud, Pythagoras
surveyed the anxious turmoil down below.
Lucretius from a similar height too:
"How sweet to contemplate a storm-tossed sea."

We know too much. We do not know enough.
We peer down, down,
try to envision the submersible
imploding halfway to the ocean's floor.

Five passengers. And more- and hundreds more-
lost when a listing overcrowded boat
packed with people hoping for a haven
capsized. What we can't see

we can imagine—cannot not imagine.
Are we complicit? And where are we?
Not on some height to contemplate the scene,
not in troubled waters down below,

but in between,
spectators, but also
the anxious crowd Pythagoras observed,
scrambling to get to where they do not know.

Our vantage point: a cloud of information,
data we both inhabit and consume,
doing what our kind have always done,
looking before and after, Hamlet said.

And also: *crawling between earth and heaven.*
Lucretius, after having called it "sweet"
to gaze at troubled waters far below,
adds "Don't think this is schadenfreude. No;

just that we savor our tranquility.
We're not the people floundering in that sea.
Ataraxia, Epicurus said:
absence of disturbance, of disorder.

Amanda Gorman calls it apathy.
In all this calm there lurks complicity.
Safe in our cloud, we listen and we look.
We calculate the numbers of the dead.

We marvel at unprecedented heat.
The storms have passed for now in this green state.
Floods have receded. Between earth and heaven
I squint up at the sky: a hazy glare.

A rainbow? Something trembles in the air.
Each hour, each minute notifications come:
storms, floods, drownings, wildfires, heat, and smoke.
Complicit in our cloud, we're keeping track.

Rachel Hadas

The day a poet is murdered by ICE

is a school day like every other
in the first week of the year.
Time isn't real but still
it's January, and scientists say
we're gaining about sixty seconds
of sunlight even as the sun sets.
I wake up and feel closer to death
than the day before. I am a mother,
so I wait for my daughter at the bottom
of the stairs and I hold her hand
when crossing the street and when
we stop at the corner I run my fingers
over her ponytail like it's my own hair.
She says there's a cloud in the sky
that looks like a heart but I can't see
what she sees. I am a mother
so when she is hungry I feed her
and when she asks me how to spell *wolves*
I explain how some nouns transform
in the plural. *Man* is *men* and *tooth* is *teeth*
and *person who is murdered* becomes *people*.

Hannah Eve Levy
Written in honor of Renee Nicole Good, a poet and a mother.

I Long to See Her Unharmed Breathing Air the Earth Is Meant to Breathe

i follow the poet

because i want
to see her

free

words make a
light path

to the country

i long to see

breathing

oxygen of cerulean skies
that all of the earth is
meant to breathe

unharmed

i will call her She
her feminine pronouns Her Hers

after violence
what does it mean

thriving

does She fold
into herself onto Herself

and after

long after the assaults

i follow the poet
he tells me to write

at my blue desk
a candle's flame
there is a window
the air smells
like snow arriving

an army

ravages
Her people and the land they belong to
the country She is

when i was a child
my father and i talked

i miss him

She exists She is
a Country
my father would say
in morocco he fought
to protect Arab
children
from the french rampage

in paris i never thought twice
when i wore my black and grey and white
scarf patterns of olive trees
passages from the sea onto Her land

i am not Palestinian but
french american from
corsica

i follow the poet
he is breaking my heart
each day

when the violence ends
how will She breathe
in Her restored cerulean sky
glimpse sun on Her
Mediterranean waters

Nathalie Canessa Kramer

¡SÍ, SE PUEDE!

What ordinary people can do in the coming months.

A youth-led climate justice group changes its focus
to combat "the billionaire cronies" who want to "turn
this country into a playground for the rich."

I'm absolutely disgusted that premiums will DOUBLE.

A congresswoman from Georgia, who once
supported the hanging of a former President,
calls for continuation of his health care benefits.

What kind of man marries somebody named Usha?

An Indian American who voted for the candidate
three times is appalled by his restriction of H1-B visas
and the hateful vitriol aimed at the VP's Indian spouse.

I thought they were only going to go after criminals.

A conservative podcaster laments, "Okay, sure, but there must be
a way to do this that doesn't involve ripping parents away from their children,
removing people who've been contributing to American society."

It takes a village to care for our children.

A teacher in Los Angeles, is working tirelessly
to bring back her high school honors student
who was deported to Guatemala with her ailing mother.

No tyrants, no dictators, no kings.

The second No Kings rally was "one of the largest single-day protests
In American history." Seven million people came out to joyously
celebrate Democracy in 2,700 American cities and towns.

YES, WE CAN!

Simki Ghebremichael

grace like time is everywhere

spilt wine's spread—white linen
plunging hawk—vacant nest

ant hefting peanut crumbs
floating leaves—the rhythm of raking

how can I not protect every little bit
of these beings
                          and don't forget stones
how currents craft their ribs

you offer me chamomile tea
                          in fine china
I wrap my arms
                  around your you

peregrine car frames contorted by boulders
serpentine cancer cell membranes

a child in point shoes—plié-fall-plié
a toddler pedaling a green tricycle

broken glass—flowering shards

Sarah B Sullivan

Besiege Your Siege

for the essayist and poet Mosab Abu Toha.

Detained and beaten
  By Israeli Defense Forces
    At the Rafa Crossing
      Between Gaza and Egypt
        Rescued by pressure
          From the world's literary community,

Your book of poems
  Things You May Find
    Hidden In My Ear

Haunts us
  With its heartbreaking
    Lived experience
      Of being alive
        In Gaza

With its shrapnel and smoke bombs,
  Infused with strawberry water
    And morning dew,
      It's refugee ruins,
        It's Palestinian pride,
          Checkpoint to checkpoint,
            Prayer to prayer.

How the wind stirs you
  With hope
    As you write

"Hope is a difficult word for Palestinians.
   It is not something that
      Others give us, but, something
         We must cultivate and care for
            On our own,
               We have to help grow hope."

Terry Hauptman

Mary

We were standing among the buildings,
what was left of the buildings,
trying to decide what to do.
It was dawn, sometime in November.
There was a scarcity of food.
Explosions of unknown origin continued
to light up the sky, confusing the many birds.
We argued, some wanting to move out in groups
with guns, others judging it best to remain
in our defensible position.
Later, under fall of night, we set out as a unit
on what was believed to be a southerly course.
But I left them, Mary, in the developing night.
I headed north to find you.

John Foy

The Country in the Mirror

1

Behind the scream pressed into headlines
behind the shouting crowd behind
the sirens behind
the ticking clock on a distant wall
                                        is a river
                        is a river
          is a river
it flows between buildings and banks
of chanting cottonwoods in the moonlight and it flows
along the spine
                        between
              left and
        right

This is where you enter the river
                here is the breath you ride
                                the boat waiting like a lover
                for your arrival and it will take you
to shore where you will find
                your footing with all your toes
                                pointing the way forward
                to the next step
and the next

2

The heart goes first
before the feet pivot
after the head turns

how to fuse the far-flung
parts of the body
into a singular motion

to inhabit the gap
between the hips that beckon
and the toes that turn back

the heart goes first
flinging itself from the cliff
and you its ancient burro

carry its remains
back up the mountain
with arms that embrace

and legs that walk away

3

As you walk you turn the earth
pulling the road under your sole
                              pushing it behind
every footprint moving mountains and the moment
you look up you find
                    the eyes you overlooked looking into

            here the shirtless
                    man behind his sign
            here the tired clerk
                    you waited for in line
            here the travelers on the train
                    praying to their phones
            here the one who holds you
                    when you circle home

Start with the country in the mirror
wherever you go
                  the long curve of the gaze
curls back to you
          since what you see
is how you look

4

Every ring on the tree every line
on your face is new growth
let others count the seasons

        your task is to arrive
        and arrive because you are
        the one who has gone

and undergone everything
inside your shoes from room
to room and storm to storm

        you have cried your way to laughter
        you have laughed your way to tears
        the line between them

disappears as the view
opens in the space you occupy
the birds swerve south

        the birds swerve north
        be still and you will turn
        home without moving

5

Close your eyes
            the woods are waiting

walk a thousand trees in
            and a thousand trees out

go down through the roots
            of the tree that once held you

its fruit in your hand
            in the chair that holds you here

your arms on its arms
            climb a thousand trees up

and a thousand trees down
            ask them how ask what now

clouds come snow comes wind
            birds squirrels and squeals

of children by the time you awaken
            you'll have outgrown the question

the trees have lost
            their leaves and show

us how to hold on
            is how to let go

6

> Do not search for it
and you will skid on it

> right on time
where it always was

> in the surprise
of the cat's leap

> the smell of coffee
and the rain

> that refutes the drought
underfoot where you're not

> looking in the last
stroke of the violin

> in the first row
of the corncob

> in the back hooves
of the wind

7

Walk a thousand steps left
and a thousand steps right
you are moving forward

out of the house you outgrew
what you put on yesterday
leg by leg and arm over arm and face

the country in the mirror
walk a thousand years in
and a thousand years out

each footprint lighter
than the last and the last
breath you take is a first
                              walking the water
                    downriver
          downriver

however you appear to disappear
through the turnstile of a thousand faces
on the trail of a thousand years

                                             Wyatt Townley

Four Years

The king goes down to the sea
and forbids the tide to wash over his feet.
It washes over them anyhow
along with two thousand years of knowledge,
science, and art, people freed
decades ago by Civil Rights movements,
and those more recently protected
by the legislation he wants to erase,
the queer and disabled.
The tide continues to wash over his feet;
it's up to his knees now.
There is a tsunami on the horizon,
a herd of horses coming up at him
out of the green dark,
ridden by ghosts of the holocaust,
of the Inquisition, of slavery.
They are the horses of history
that will trample everything but
the faintest stain of him,
the unfortunate recrudescence
of every Caligula rerun, the Hitlers,
the Pol Pots, the Stalins,
the battalions of sycophants
the embarrassing hucksters and snake oil salesmen.
He shouts but the thunder of hooves drowns him out.
Does he actually think that much truth
can be hidden, expunged?
That the world is not watching him,
that Europe, steeped in centuries of gore,
does not recognize his foul spectacle?
Now the water is up to his chin.
He flails around in it but it is sweeping
the sand from under his feet.
It will lift him in its great swell

and carry him away. It takes four years,
but there he goes.
The orcas are tracking him.
He is in the Antarctic now, being frozen in time.
Dante would have put him in lowest bolgia,
the festering ice between Satan's feet.
There he is, the last snarl of contempt
frozen on his face,
and the deluge of history closes over him.

Doug Anderson

Dare

Headlines
too horrendous
to be real
assault my eyes
from screens
that hold me captive.
Look away,
my heart screams,
but my brain
orders me to
CONSUME
IT
ALL.
It fears missing
something important
to survival,
like a call to flee
the chaos
created by con men,
criminals,
and villainous characters
that belong on the pages
of comic books
and not in positions
of power.
Atrocities accumulate,
and I become frantic,
scrolling past,
clicking away,
searching for hope
in a digital realm
that doesn't even
tell the truth

anymore.
My gaze grows weary.
I close my eyes,
and listen,
just listen,
to my breathing,
my heartbeat,
the small voice
inside my head
that whispers,
All is not lost.
And I remember
that hope dwells
in each of us.
If we don't like
the headlines,
we can rewrite them.
If we don't like
the characters,
we can recast them.
If we don't like
the atrocities,
we can stop them.
We, the people,
can create
the best version
of reality
if we simply
dare to dream,
to believe,
to act
with love.

Christine DePetrillo

"The Survivors' Revolution"

Press conference, November 18, 2025, US Capitol, before the House
of Representatives vote to release Epstein files.

On the Capitol steps, women once girls,
young teens exploited, assaulted, harmed
by powerful men, masters of finance,
now call for truth, a survivors' revolution.

Young teens exploited, assaulted, harmed,
trapped by lies of bright and safe futures,
now call for truth, a survivors' revolution,
vengeance against the deceivers, the users

whose lies of bright and safe futures,
turned innocent girlhood to sorrow.
Revenge against the deceivers, the users,
the shouts of RELEASE THE FILES!

for all whose innocence turned to sorrow
ring across the land, across the world.
The shout, RELEASE THE EPSTEIN FILES!
brings shame onto the heads of the guilty,

disrupts unholy power in the land, across the world,
brings princes down, erases their unearned privilege,
marks SHAME upon their foreheads. GUILTY!
The girls, the women who will not be quiet,

confront princes, presidents, erase that unearned privilege.
Let their voices rise, our voices rise. RELEASE THE FILES!
cry the girls, the women who will not be quiet.
They raise the plea for all the girls, for our daughters,

for ourselves. Let voices shout RELEASE THE FILES!

Let those who use power to hide their rotten faces
hear the plea for all our girls—all our children!
Let them see their shriveled selves, let them burn,

all those who've used power to hide their rotten faces,
weak "powerful" men, masters of deceit and finance.
We'll watch them shrink, resized and small, burn
on the Capitol steps, brought down by women, once girls.

Sharon Darrow

Well Being

Let us be known
for the plea, sea to sea—one country,
lakes, plains, city streets,
essential work rewarded
long past pandemic disease.
Fairness regardless of skin or origin,
inequity's truth an epiphany,
warding off war again.

Let us be known
for Lincoln and King,
for questioning, inventing,
justice boring through
smokescreens, through hate
berating those dragging their bones
as the richest gain riches.

Let us be known
for opposing those
who sharpen their claws
on our daughters' plea
for a new economy
steeped in well-being.

Let us be known
for clearing the sky for better lives,
now and then—an extra slice of pie,
known for the falcons' wingbeat
freeing seas of hungry children
as the raptor's shadow passes,
dropping bills like uneaten seeds.

Judith Janoo

Poets

The poets are the last hope.

When the door is slammed shut
The poet's fingers will bleed.

When the gavel cracks down hard on the bench
The poets will not sit down
And they will not stop talking.

When the stranger moans in ugly agony
The poets alone will pause
Amidst the many footsteps stiffly walking away.

Poetry is the last bastion.

Against the anguish and the loneliness
Against the algorithms of the apocalypse
Against the devils devouring our world.

When the clamorous clueless march to the cliff
The poets will cry out
With rhymes for the righteous
With couplets of compassion
With unrepentant lyrics of love.

Pete Blose

Poetic Justice

I don't throw punches,
I throw lines—
crafted like daggers,
softened like rhymes.
My weapon's my voice,
not the heat of my fist,
I conquer the hate
with a flick of my wrist.

In a world that slanders
with venomous speech,
I answer with verses
that teach what fists can't reach.
They hurl their shade
like stones in the dark,
I turn pain to poetry,
and scars into art.

Each stanza's a stance,
each metaphor's might,
I don't brawl in the streets,
I make wrongs write.
They may bruise my name,
try to bury my truth,
but I spit revolution
like fire in the booth.

I've seen battles
where silence was loss,
but I learned to wage war
without bearing the cost.
No bars, no cuffs,
no regrets in my wake—
just echoes of justice

in each breath I take.
So I rise with my ink,
steady and bold,
turning trials to tales
that forever get told.
And when life tries to choke me,
to drown out my sound—
I rhyme louder,
till my words shake the ground.

Because peace isn't passive—
it's power restrained,
it's speaking with purpose
when you're tempted by pain.
Let them swing blindly,
I'll still choose the pen—
'cause fighting with wisdom
makes me greater than men.

Amanda Harris

Symphony in Hope Major

In the coming year, I hope to hear,
our village orchestra loud and clear.
Maraca cicadas, rasping bees,
children playing timpani,
and in the morning's hurry-up rush
tooting skylarks and fluting thrush.
The violin plunk-plop raindrops bring,
snowbell and bluebells' ting-a-ling,
saucy woodpeckers' castanets,
humming birds buzzing like mini jets,
honking clarinets gliding home,
orange sunsets' slide trombone,
sousaphone grouse, whale's bassoon,
snowflake confetti kissing the moon.
In the coming year I hope to hear
a joyous symphony, loud and clear.

Kelly Bennett

The World up Close

When everything true
seems too far away, or
permanently missing in action,
bring your face in close.

Be near-sighted
with the world.
Each single thing is every
single thing, so tell me,

who do you see? What
do you smell? Do you
hear that? It's you
making sense of it all.

Once you know this street
sign, this pine
needle, this bird's
song, high-pitched giggle

of your neighbor's youngest
walking to school each morning,
you will know everything. Mostly
you will know yourself

as you stretch, sob, sing,
near-sighted as can be, leaning
in close, closer, to love
the smallest thing.

cin salach

The Allegory of Elms

What I remember from childhood
was not so much their stateliness—their
hallelujahs of upward limbs parading
in procession up the long avenues—

but the day they came down: how the tall
plumb ranks they formed suddenly tumbled
into jumbles of sticks and stumps, and the for-
granted shade they gave left forever,

so even the cloudiness of that day
had the blinding effect of making
the world too bright to really see.

Decades later, I found one last tree, alone,
in a field, its limbs lifting the air back up
as if extinction were incomplete.

Tim Mayo

A Gathering

for Baron Wormser

Safe as we are here, awakened
To fear: bludgeoned by news,
Top of the hour.
Set the coffee to steep, let's go
Down the dawn-facing slope
Ankling through meadowsweet,

Free-seeding thyme and oregano,
Tented webs in wet grass.
An early haze, like steam. Or smoke.
There, our bushes in a patch,
Nine paces by four, laden
with hundreds of blueberries.

Wearied and appalled,
The traffic of slaughter seen or heard
Glancingly, from a corner of the mind,
But listen, the double trochee couplets
Of a mourning warbler at woods' edge,
Knell of a windchime in easy breeze.

Let loose a moan, a groan, a sigh,
Still the berries are glossy blue,
Soft droplet of taste with a spark of sour.

We'll start at the near side and go east,
Search among leaves, a quiet feast.
As minutes pass, more fruit
Seems ripened back where we began.
Slip them into pail or mouth.
Grief gives way.

By this, occupied:
Little blue globes
Between forefinger and thumb.
Eased enough, could we say?
To once more
begin.

Jim Schley

N'envoyez pas de fleurs

"La haine tue toujours, l'amour ne meurt jamais."
—Mahatma Gandhi

Une vaste toile se tisse.

Tout le monde le sait.

Tout le monde le sent.

Déjà, on en devine les premiers fils sur l'horizon des temps à venir et le ciel de nos futurs revêt un peu plus chaque jour les tons et les couleurs des innombrables pertes et des nombreux deuils qui nous attendent.

Il y a quelque chose de pourri au royaume de la post-vérité et du mensonge; le nouveau souverain réclame un empire.

Belzébuth lorgne du côté de ma maison. L'enfer est son domaine et le malheur son bon plaisir.

Des jours d'intolérance et de mépris s'alignent dans le destin des êtres encore à être, dans un monde où naître ou ne pas naître n'est souvent plus une option, où être ou ne pas être n'est pas la question.

Un monde où tout est noir ou blanc, dont les tons de gris sont désormais bannis, et qui délave, qui dégrade et puis efface les couleurs et les nuances trop subtiles du fier arc-en-ciel de ses propres enfants.

Non, n'envoyez pas de fleurs

Tracez plutôt à la plume ou au crayon l'image d'un rêve, d'un souhait, d'une montagne à gravir, d'un sommet à conquérir afin de pouvoir contempler le monde dans toute sa splendeur. Car il sera toujours là, offrant à la vue de qui osera, ses plus beaux horizons et ses plus prometteuses perspectives sur tous les possibles des années encore à venir. Tournons ensemble la page d'une Histoire déjà marquée par tant de siècles de violence, mais féconde et porteuse de jours de bonté et de beauté offerts à qui saura se les approprier.

Bien sûr, la route qui mène au mieux passe souvent par le pire, mais un nouveau matin n'est-il jamais plus lumineux que comparé à la noire solitude de la nuit qui l'a précédé et la grâce d'un bonheur n'en devient-elle pas plus précieuse quand elle adoucit de nombreux et douloureux soucis ?

Ouvrons les portes de l'armoire aux souhaits et le tiroir de nos plus beaux secrets où dorment les semences de jours meilleurs, n'attendant que la naissance d'un prochain printemps qui, n'en doutons pas, refleurira un jour.

Exprimons en mots sur une page, en notes sur une portée, en couleurs sur une toile le projet tant caressé pour le meilleur et contre le pire, qui ne demande qu'à voir le jour.

Ensemble, permettons à nos rêves de rêver grand, de rêver beau.

N'envoyez pas de fleurs

Cherchons la beauté au cœur de la tempête. L'imagination garde encore sa place dans le grand cours de l'Histoire. Chaque vie, même infime, fait pencher le monde de son souffle. Donnons corps à nos idéaux les plus hauts et ensemble décidons de la suite du monde.

Demain commence déjà dans la pensée. Chaque despote porte une fissure cachée, chaque tyran rencontre sa fin. La volonté ferme les fait ployer, le courage les abat.

Ensemble, nous détenons le véritable pouvoir.

Martin Luther King avait un rêve. Gandhi avait un rêve.

Rêvons, nous aussi, ... mais les yeux grands ouverts.

Jean-Blaise Bourque

Do Not Send Flowers

"Hatred ever kills, love never dies."—Mahatma Gandhi

A giant web is expanding.

Everybody knows it.

We can all feel it.

Already the horizon glimmers with the faint threads of days to come, and the sky of our tomorrows slowly gathers the muted colors of losses that await.

Something is rotting in the realm of "alternative facts," where falsehood crowns itself king and demands an empire.

Beelzebub is at my doorstep. Misery is his language and ruin his pleasure.

Days heavy with contempt settle on the fate of those not yet shaped by life, in a world where being born is no longer a choice and where the question of being loses all meaning.

A world stripped of gray, sharpened into black and white only, washing away the tender spectrum of its own children's rainbow until their true colours fall silent.

No, do not send flowers

Send instead the stroke of a pen, the trace of a dream sketched on paper, the ascent of a mountain imagined at dawn. Offer the vision of a summit from which the world might once again reveal its splendor. The world will still be there, patient, generous, opening its wide horizons to those who dare open their eyes. Let us turn the heavy page of a History carved by centuries of wounds, yet still rich with mornings of tenderness for those who choose to gather them.

The road toward light often crosses fields of darkness.
Yet no dawn glows brighter than the one born after deep night, and
no joy shines truer than the one that lays its balm upon long-carried
sorrow.

Open the cabinet where forgotten wishes sleep.
Open the drawer where lie secret hopes, the seeds of better days
that rest trusting the return of a spring season that never breaks its
promise.

Give them voice on paper, color on canvas, music in the air.
Give shape to the quiet vision that longs to enter the world.
Let our dreams rise immense, luminous, unafraid.

Do not send flowers

Search for beauty inside the storm. Imagination still holds its sacred
place in the great current of History. Every life, even the smallest, tilts
the world by a breath. Give life to your highest ideals.
Choose the shape of things to come.

Tomorrow begins already inside the mind. Every despot bears a
hidden fracture. Every tyrant meets an end. Faced with determination
and persistence they can only bend or fall.
Together we hold the true power.

Martin Luther King had a dream. Gandhi had a dream.

Let us dream too ... but with our eyes wide open.

Jean-Blaise Bourque

Cut Flowers

a yellow
  petal falls
    from the jar
of tulips
  onto the
    blue woolen
shawl woven
  with masses
    of flowers
scrambling
  along the
    frayed border

outside it's
  snowing it
    keeps snowing
the petals
  keep falling
    the flowers
keep growing

Susan Gillis

Mourning Dove

who calls from the emergent pine
across the tidal slough
I hands cupped my thumbs together respond
that low lonely call of the hope
and he calls back flies closer
I am here at the end of my time
and he alone searching for others of his kind
I call again and he responds
flies to the maple thicket
carried by our chorus
so we both perch-call-wait
calling for comfort
calling for mate

in these times
we become both the caller and called
for if we no longer sing
what becomes of us all

Bill Pendergraft

All of Us, Singing

> *This is the sound of all of us*
> *Singing with love and the will to trust*
> —from "One Voice" by The Wailin' Jennys

This is the sound of all of us, singing
together like a flock of fervent birds
pitching forward against the dark winds
until we're listened to, until we land

together like a flock of fervent birds
a storm of our own making, singing
until we're listened to, until we land
We are unweary and unafraid

a storm of our own making, singing
pitching forward against the dark winds
We are unweary and unafraid
This is the sound of all of us, singing

Liz Garton Scanlon

Acknowledgments

I am grateful to friends and family who encouraged me and supported me in this project, and to the dedicated poets in our protest and witness workshop in March when we saw how difficult the days were becoming and would likely be for some time. Their courage and honesty helped me realize that poets have something to say about what is happening in our country and our world, and that our voices need to be heard. I'm grateful to Madeleine who offered space for the workshop to meet; to Martha, who gave poets months of Open Mic gallery space to read our works and who graciously allowed us to use her beautiful art for this book's cover; to Catamount Arts' Poetry Potluck Open Mic and Sarah for a place to gather; to Anne for her encouragement and belief in this project; to Tara Lynn and the early morning group that sparked the idea in the first place. I am grateful, too, to the Barton Wednesday Poets and the Poetry Society of Vermont, courageous poets all. I am grateful for and in awe of all the poets who have lent their poems and voices to this anthology. A huge measure of gratitude also goes to Samantha Kolber and Rootstock Publishing for their belief and partnership in this endeavor, a good work. Most of all, I am grateful every day for my husband Jerry and his support and love. Without him, none of this would have happened. He makes my wishes come true.

Credits

Grateful acknowledgment goes to the editors who previously published the following poets:

John Foy: "Mary" in *At Play*, Kelsay Books, 2024.

Susan Gillis: "Cut Flowers" in *Poets Reading the News*, March 2022.

Rachel Hadas: "The Truth as Well" in *Literary Matters*; "Fire and Flood and Bureau Drawer" in *The Hudson Review*; "The Truth as Well" in *Birmingham Poetry Review*, spring, 2026.

Terry Hauptman: "The Bataan Death March" and "Besiege Your Siege" in *Shattered*, North Star Press, 2025.

Paul Hoover: "The Dry Bones" in *Poetry*, March 2011; "Signs and Wonders" in *Greening the Earth: A Global Anthology*, Vintage 2024; *Winter in America*, ed. Roxi Power, Carbonation Press, 2025; and the *Ampersand Review*, 2013; "As a Lion in Secret Places" in *Warwick Review*, December 2010.

Judith Janoo: "Neighbor" in *The Townships Sun*, 2025; "Edge of the Gorge" in *Pedestal Magazine*, 2022; "Take to the Streets, February 15, 2003" in *After Effects*, Finishing Line Press, 2019; "The Still Small Possibility" in *Main Street Rag*, 2026; "Well Being" in *The Mountain Troubadour*, Poetry Society of Vermont, and *Just This*, Kelsay Books, 2023;

David M. Katz: "The Green of Greenland" in *Poetry in Performance 53*, CCNY Poetry Outreach Center, 2025.

Samantha Kolber: "It's the Beginning of the End and I'm Here to Tell You" in *PoemCity Anthology 2025*, Rootstock Publishing.

Tricia Knoll: "I-89 from Vermont to Canada in Winter" in *The New Verse News*, March, 2025.

Tim Mayo: "The Allegory of Elms" as "The Legacy of Elms" in *Rat's Ass Review*, summer 2019.

Mary Meriam: "Forest" in The Nature of Our Times, 2025; "Hunger" in *Poetry X Hunger*, 2025.

Steve Minkin: "Shoelaces" in *Moral Oblivion*, Kelsay Books, 2025.

Sean Prentiss: "On the Day of the Election, I Think of the Video of My Nephew's First Mountain Bike Ride with His Father, a Long Haul Covid Survivor" in *Crayfish Magazine*, Vol 2.

Bianca Stone: "The Way Things Were Up Until Now" in *What Is Otherwise Infinite*, Tin House, 2022 and *The New Yorker*, 2021.

Wyatt Townley: "The Country in the Mirror," commissioned by Unity Church, in *The Midwest Quarterly*, 2023 and in *Making the Turn*, Lost Horse Press, 2026.

Contributors

Kauakanilehua Māhoe Adams is a mixed Native Hawaiian author, and poet with an MFA in Writing for Children and Young Adults from Vermont College of Fine Arts. She was a finalist for the 2025 Steve Kowit Poetry Prize and is the author of *An Expanse of Blue*, a young adult novel in verse.

Pamela Ahlen is special events coordinator for Osher Lifelong Learning Institute at Dartmouth. Pamela is the author of the chapbook *Gather Every Little Thing* (Finishing Line Press) and the co-author (with Anne Bower) of *Getting it Down on Paper, Shaping a Friendship* (Orchard Street Press).

Amy Allen, Poet Laureate of Shelburne, Vermont, is the author of *Mountain Offerings* (2024). Her work explores the intersection of nature and human experience and appears in numerous literary journals. She also owns All of the Write Words, a freelance writing and editing service.

Doug Anderson's most recent book is *Undress, She Said*, from Four Way Books. His *New and Selected Poems* will be published by Saturnalia Books in 2026. He has recent work in *Cutthroat*.

Alexander Anlyan spent twenty-three years working for public mental health during the day and teaching convicted felons anger management two evenings a week. His life has centered around personal growth, spirituality, and poetry. His writing reflects observations of personal transformation in response to the changing world.

Kathi Appelt has written over sixty books, including *The Underneath*, a National Book Award finalist, and a Newbery Honor. She lives in College Station, Texas with her husband and cats. She has recently taken up boxing.

Kelly Bennett writes for children—mostly picture books celebrating all that goes into being a kid...and baseball! These include *Not Norman, Norman One Amazing Goldfish, Rainbow Kite, The House That Ruth Built*, and *Out of the Mouth of Babe*. Kelly is a weed picking, two-wheeler based in Westhampton Beach, New York.

Julie Berry is the *New York Times* bestselling author of *If Looks Could Kill*, the 2020 NCTE Walden Award and SCBWI Golden Kite Award winner *Lovely War*, and the 2017 Printz Honor *The Passion of Dolssa*. Julie holds an MFA from Vermont College and owns Author's Note, a bookstore in historic Medina, New York.

Meredith Bergmann is an award-winning public sculptor, and a filmmaker, essayist and critic. Her poetry has appeared widely in journals and anthologies. Her chapbook *A Special Education*, is available online from Bainbridge Island Press, and *The Dying Flush* (2024), with poetry and illustrations by Bergmann, is available from EXOT Books.

James Bird is a Gichi-Onigaming (Grand Portage band of Lake Superior Ojibwe) author and filmmaker. He has published four award-winning middle grade novels—*The Brave, The Second Chance of Benjamin Waterfalls, No Place Like Home*, and *Wolf Club*—and has written and directed five films. When he's not writing or on set, he spends his time with his *New York Times* bestselling author wife Adriana Mather and their son, Wolf, rescuing animals.

Pete Blose offers this thought: B.Traven once said biography means nothing. Only the writing counts.

Stephen Bluestone has won the Thomas Merton Prize and the Greensboro Review Prize and published three volumes of poetry, the latest of which was *The Painted Clock* (Mercer University Press, 2018). He also co-edited and co-translated a bilingual anthology of the poetry of Mexico City and New York City, *From Neza York to New York*. Work has appeared in *Poetry, The Sewanee Review, The Hudson Review, Boston Review*, and other journals.

Jean-Blaise Bourque, a retired translator born and raised in Quebec, spent most of his professional life serving the Canadian Government, shaping language and playing with words. Ever attentive to the world around him, he realizes more each day that one must be able to lend an ear in order to listen, and learn to listen in order to understand.

Louella Bryant is author of eleven award-winning books of fiction and nonfiction. Her stories, essays, and poems have appeared in lit mags and anthologies, including *Southern Sin* (Creative Nonfiction Foundation). Formerly on the faculty of Spalding University and University of Vermont, she now works as an independent editor.

S. J. Cahill lives and writes in Vermont's Northeast Kingdom where albino wolves and unicorns are frequently sighted.

Mary Cheyne lives in Chelsea, Vermont with lots of furry friends. She has been writing poetry for about three years now. She says it is an honor to have her poems included in this anthology.

daithí (he/him) lives with his wife in Montpelier on the unceded land of the Abenaki people. He has published in *Tendril, Refocus* and in recent *Mountain Troubadour* publications. His ancestral home rests primarily on what is now called Ireland.

Sharon Darrow, award-winning author of picture books for children and novels for young adults, and whose poems, short stories, interviews, and personal essays for adults have appeared in literary journals and anthologies, was a member of the writing faculty of Vermont College of Fine Arts for over twenty years.

Chard deNiord is the author of nine books of poetry, most recently *Westminster West* (Tupelo Press, 2025), *One As Other* (Green Writers Press), and *In My Unknowing* (University of Pittsburgh Press 2020). He served as the Poet Laureate of Vermont from 2015 to 2019.

Christine DePetrillo can be found hugging trees, conversing with dragonflies, and walking barefoot through sun-warmed soil. She is a romance author and poet who finds inspiration in nature. Her fictional tales will make you laugh, maybe make you sweat, and definitely make you believe in the power of love.

Arlene Iris Distler has been writing for forty years. A chapbook, *Voices Like Wind Chimes*, was published by Finishing Line press in 2014, and a full-length book of poems, *This Earth, This Body*, was published in 2022 by Kelsay Books. Distler's poems have appeared in numerous anthologies. She is co-founder of Write Action, a nonprofit for writers.

Aria Dominguez's poetry and creative nonfiction navigate the terrain between beauty and pain. She won the 2021 Porch Prize in Creative Nonfiction, a Fall 2021 Brooklyn Poets Fellowship, and the 2022 Sunlight Press Essay Contest. She was awarded a Minnesota State Arts Board Creative Individuals grant in 2024 and 2025. Aria works with a nonprofit focused on food justice and lives in Saint Paul.

Born in Querétaro, Mexico, **Raúl Dorantes** immigrated to Chicago in 1986. He has been involved with several literary magazines and currently serves on the editorial board of *El Beisman*. He co-authored an essay collection, *Y nos vinimos de mojados*, with Febronio Zatarain. He is an award-winning playwright and a professor of Latin American literature at Northeastern Illinois University.

Born in Connecticut in 1943, **Sandy Edmonds** has often passed through her home state on the way to Vermont from New York stopping there occasionally, always interested in its troubling underbelly. Yet pulled more by family, animals and gardening, she finds peace in the other two destinations.

Martín Espada's latest book of poems is called *Jailbreak of Sparrows*. His previous book of poems, *Floaters*, won the National Book Award. He has received the Ruth Lilly Poetry Prize, the Shelley Memorial Award, a Letras Boricuas Fellowship and a Guggenheim Fellowship. He teaches at the University of Massachusetts-Amherst.

Cindy Faughnan writes poems for children and adults which have appeared in *Roar Kids Magazine*, *Dirigible Balloon*, *High Five*, *Tyger Tyger Magazine*, and *Visual Verse*. She completed an MFA in Writing for Children and Young Adults at Vermont College of Fine Arts.

John Foy's fourth book of poems, *At Play*, was published last year by Kelsay Books. His third book, *No One Leaves the World Unhurt*, won the Donald Justice Poetry Prize (Autumn House Press, 2021). His work has been published widely in journals and online.

Jennifer Franklin is a poet, professor, and editor. She is the author of four poetry collections including *A Fire in Her Brain* (Princeton University Press, 2026). She has received a Pushcart Prize, a grant from NYFA, and a residency from the T.S. Eliot Foundation. She teaches online manuscript revision workshops and in Manhattanville's MFA program.

Elizabeth Fred lives in Northern Vermont.

Robin Galbraith lives near Washington, DC and has two adult children. She did not go to all the work of making and raising them so that they would have fewer rights than she did. Thus, she spends a lot of time protesting at the White House. She has an MFA from Vermont College of Fine Arts.

Simki Ghebremichael received her MFA from American University. Her poem "Prague TV" was awarded first prize by Split This Rock. Her writing has appeared in *Potomac Review, Passager*, and *Capitalism, Nature, Socialism*. Her book, *Pauli Murray's Revolutionary Life*, was published by Rootstock Publishing in 2022 under her married name, Simki Kuznick.

Joanne Giannino lives in Westmore, Vermont with her husband. A lifelong writer, she is an active member of the Barton Wednesday Poets. Her articles, poems and essays have appeared in a variety of anthologies and magazines. Her chapbook, *Journey Woman Poems*, was published with a Massachusetts Cultural Council grant.

Susan Gillis has lived on the Atlantic and Pacific coasts of Canada and in Tiotià:ke Montréal, and now makes her home in Algonquin territory near Perth, Ontario.

Rigoberto González is the editor of *Latino Poetry*, a Library of America anthology. He received the 2025 Ruth Lilly Award for Lifetime Achievement in Poetry from the Poetry Foundation. He's currently distinguished professor at the MFA program in Creative Writing at Rutgers-Newark.

Shalom Gorewitz (b.1949) is a pioneering video artist, curator, and writer whose work bridges image processing and social commentary. A Guggenheim Fellow and former curator at The Kitchen, he collaborated with dancers like Daniel Nagrin and has exhibited internationally while continuing to explore experimental media and poetry. He lives in New York City and Danville, Vermont with his wife Rachel Hadas.

Chris Solís Green is the author of five books of poetry, most recently *The Dead Zoo* (Bee Box Press, 2025). He's edited numerous anthologies, including *American Gun: A Poem by 100 Chicagoans* and *Chicago Mosaic: Immigrant Stories of Objects Kept, Lost, or Left Behind*. He's a Distinguished Writer in Residence at DePaul University.

New York Times bestseller **Nikki Grimes** received the ALAN Award for teen literature, Children's Literature Legacy Medal, NCTE Award for Excellence in Poetry for Children, and the Coretta Scott King Award. A Black Authors Hall of Fame Inductee, her titles include *Bronx Masquerade, Garvey's Choice*, and *Ordinary Hazards: A Memoir*.

Adrienne Gruber (she/her) is an award-winning author of three books of poetry. Her first book of essays, *Monsters, Martyrs, and Marionettes: Essays on Motherhood* was published with Book*hug in 2024. She lives with her partner and their three daughters on Nex̱wlélex̱m (Bowen Island), the traditional lands of the Squamish Nation.

The author of many books of poetry, essays, and translations, **Rachel Hadas** has been a Guggenheim fellow in poetry, among other honors. Professor Emerita of English at the Newark campus of Rutgers University, she lives in New York City and Danville, Vermont. Her latest collection is *Pastorals* (Measure Press 2025).

Amanda Harris is a young woman from California who found her voice on the page when the world refused to hear it aloud. Writing became the doorway to her truth, where silence broke, and people finally stopped to listen. Through poetry, she transforms pain into power and speaks for the versions of herself once unheard.

Shattered is **Terry Hauptman**'s eighth full length volume of poetry. She holds a masters degree in Poetry, University of New Mexico, where she studied with Joy Harjo—and a PhD in interdisciplinary Arts, Ohio University. She reads her poetry rhapsodically and exhibits her luminous Songline Scrolls nationally. She has taught world art, poetry and ethnopoetics at universities and workshops, most recently at Green Mountain College.

Louise Hawes (louisehawes.com) is the author of two short fiction collections and over a dozen novels, including *The Language of Stars* (Simon & Schuster), a novel in playscripts, poetry and prose. Louise helped found the MFA Program in Writing for Children and Young Adults at VCFA, where she is currently the Katherine Paterson Chair of Children's Literature.

Mary Hawley is a poet, fiction writer, and literary translator (Spanish to English). Her poems and short stories have appeared in *Hypertext*, *The Plentitudes*, and elsewhere, and she received an Illinois Literary Award in fiction. Her translations of poetry and prose have appeared in *The Common*, *TriQuarterly*, and other journals. She lives in Evanston, Illinois.

Paul Hoover has published sixteen books of poetry, most recently, *O, and Green: New and Selected Poems* (Mad Hat Press, 2021). He is editor of two editions of *Postmodern American Poetry: A Norton Anthology* and the annual poetry magazine, *New American Writing*.

Susen James was born, so they say, on a full moon eclipse. Maybe that explains her oddness. She writes poetry & lies because she fears drifting into memoir—truthful but incomplete. When not writing, Susen can be found wandering cemeteries & woodlands or teaching her favorite students at Columbia College in Chicago Poetry Writing, Mythology & Fantasy Literature.

Judith Janoo won the Soul-Making Keats Award and the Anita McAndrews Prize for Human Rights Poetry. Her poetry has appeared in journals including *Pedestal* and the *Fish Anthology*, and in two collections, *Just This*, published by Kelsay Books, and *After Effects*, published by Finishing Line Press.

Beth Kanell (bethkanell.blogspot.com) lives in northeastern Vermont among rivers, rocks, and a lot of writers. Her poems seek comfortable seats in small well-lit places, including *The Comstock Review*, *Indianapolis Review*, *Gyroscope Review*, and *RockPaperPoem*. Her collection *Thresholds* is due in early 2026 from Kelsay Books.

David M. Katz (davidmkatzpoet.com) is the author of *The Biographer, In Praise of Manhattan, Stanzas on Oz, and Claims of Home* (Dos Madres Press), and *The Warrior in the Forest* (House of Keys). He starred in *Gully's Paradise*, a film by Shalom Gorewitz.

Garret Keizer is the author of the poetry collection *The World Pushes Back* and a contributing editor of *Harper's Magazine* and *Virginia Quarterly Review*. His poems have appeared in *Best American Poetry, Harvard Review, Raritan, The Hudson Review,* and *The New Yorker.* He lives with his wife in northeastern Vermont.

Tricia Knoll's (triciaknoll.com) poetry appears widely in journals as diverse as *New Verse News* and *Kenyon Review.* Nine collections range from full-length to chapbook. *Wild Apples* (2024, Fernwood Press) focuses on aging in Vermont. Knoll is a Contributing Editor to Verse Virtual.

Samantha Kolber (samanthakolber.com) is the author of a chapbook, *Birth of a Daughter* (Kelsay Books, 2020), and has had poems in *Rattle, Hunger Mountain,* and other journals and anthologies. Originally from Plainsboro, New Jersey, she lives in Montpelier, Vermont where she runs Rootstock Publishing and writes in her spare time. Her debut novel *What She Stole* releases in December 2026.

Originally from Singapore, **Jee Leong Koh** is a writer, editor, and publisher based in New York City. His poetry collection *Steep Tea* (Carcanet) was named a *Financial Times* Best Book of the Year and a Lambda Finalist. His work of hybrid fiction *Snow at 5 PM* won the Singapore Literature Prize.

Nathalie Canessa Kramer was born in Paris and grew up in France and California. Her writing has appeared in *Santa Monica Review, Faultline, Mediterranean Poetry, Bloodroot,* among others. She received her MFA in Fiction from Bennington College, and fellowships from Orion Environmental Writers Workshop, Writing By Writers, Disquiet Literary Prize. She completed her studies in creative nonfiction with Mountain View MFA.

Madeleine May Kunin, first woman elected governor of Vermont (three terms), also US Ambassador to Switzerland and US Deputy Secretary of Education, has written four books of poetry and four other books including *Living a Political Life* (Knopf), and *The New Feminist Agenda: Defining the Next Revolution for Women, Work, and Family,* a *New York Times* Editor's Choice. Currently James March Professor-at-Large at the University of Vermont, she lectures on feminism and politics.

Julie Larios is a poet who lives reassuringly close to the Canadian border in Bellingham, Washington. Her poems have appeared in *The Atlantic* and other magazines, as well as twice being selected for *The Best American Poetry.* She is working on a collection of poems tentatively titled *A Woman, Observed.*

Ron Lay-Sleeper (BA and MA in English, University of Connecticut) writes in the realm of metaphoric eco poetry as described by David Hinton in *The Wilds of Poetry,* and by Mary Karr in *The Art of Memoir,* as "...a fiction writer starts with meaning and then manufactures events to represent it; a memoirist starts with events, then derives meaning from them."

Author of twenty-seven books, founding editor of *New England Review*, former Pulitzer finalist and Vermont Poet Laureate, **Sydney Lea** was awarded the Governor's Award for Excellence in the Arts in 2021, his home state's highest arts distinction. His sixteenth collection of poems is *What Shines* (2023), and his second novel *Now Look* (2024).

Hannah Levy is a poet living in Berkeley, California. She's the editor-in-chief of *The Rebis*, an annual print anthology that celebrates the connection between tarot, art, and creative writing. When she's not typing little words on a screen, she's hiking in the redwoods, horseback riding, and playing extensive make-believe games with her daughter.

Amanda West Lewis (amandawestlewis.com) is a writer, theatre artist, and arts educator who specializes in work for and with young people. She is the author of award-winning novels, picture books, and poetry. Her work reflects a desire to explore the choices people make as they face challenges in their lives.

Gregory Maguire is a lifelong advocate of the significance of literature in the lives of children. He has written fiction for children, teens, and adults. His best-known work is *Wicked: The Life and Times of the Wicked Witch of the West*, which inspired the Broadway musical and the films of the same name.

Amit Majmudar, former first Poet Laureate of Ohio, is a diagnostic nuclear radiologist in Ohio. Recent and forthcoming books include *Twin A: A Memoir* (Slant Books, 2023), *The Great Game: Essays on Poetics* (Acre Books, 2024), *Three Metamorphoses: Novellas in Prose and Verse* (Orison Books, 2025), and *Things my Grandmother Said: Poems* (Knopf, 2026).

Tim Mayo's poems have received seven Pushcart Prize nominations. His second volume of poems, *Thesaurus of Separation* (Phoenicia Publishing, Montréal, 2016) was a finalist for the 2017 Montaigne Medal and for the Eric Hoffer Book Award. His collection *Muscle Memories of Love and Disaster* is hopefully forthcoming in 2026.

Alison McGhee (alisonmcghee.com) is the *New York Times* bestselling writer of novels, poems, and picture books for all ages. Her work has been translated into more than twenty languages and she's received many awards and fellowships. She lives in Minneapolis, is frequently on the road, and teaches via Zoom.

Mary Meriam's most recent poetry collection is *Pools of June* (Exot Books, 2022). Her poems have appeared in *Literary Imagination*, *Literary Matters*, *Poetry*, *Prelude*, *Subtropics*, and *The Poetry Review*.

Steve Minkin has written for both scientific and popular outlets on a range of subjects including ecological issues, health, politics and epidemiology. His latest poetry book *Moral Oblivion* concerns wars, injustices, and crimes against humanity. It joins *Where People Are Trees*, both published by Kelsay Books.

Katie Moritz is a published poet and short story writer. Her short story "The Tooth" has been nominated for a Pushcart Prize. She is working on her first book and currently lives in Vermont's rural Northeast Kingdom.

Erika Nichols-Frazer of Waitsfield, Vermont, is the author of *Feed Me: A Story of Food, Love and Mental Illness* (memoir) and *Staring Too Closely* (poems). Her short story collection, *No One Will Ever Hear You,* and poetry chapbook, *Can you see her, the moon?* will be published in 2026.

JPayne is a Northeast Kingdom native who resides in Winooski, Vermont. He is virtually unpublished. He primarily writes "voice poems" that are meant to be read aloud and has returned to writing and reading aloud after a long hiatus. In the 1990s he was a featured reader at Burlington's Fire House poets' space.

Bill Pendergraft founded Environmental Media in 1988 to write and produce environmental education content. His second book of poetry, *Love in the Age of Loneliness,* is available at environmentalmedia.com.

Sean Prentiss is the author of *Finding Abbey: the Search for Edward Abbey and His Hidden Desert Grave,* which won the National Outdoor Book Award. He has also written *Crosscut: Poems* and co-written two textbooks, *Environmental and Nature Writing* and *Advanced Creative Nonfiction.* He is a professor at Norwich University. He and his family live on a small lake in Northern Vermont.

Mike Puican's debut book of poetry is *Central Air* (Northwestern Press, 2020). He's had poems in *Poetry, Michigan Quarterly Review, Rhino, New England Review,* won the Tia Chucha Chapbook Contest for *30 Seconds,* was a member of Chicago Slam Team, president emeritus of Guild Literary Complex, and he currently teaches writing to incarcerated individuals at the Federal Metropolitan Correctional Center in Chicago.

Freelance writer and editor **Katherine Quimby** holds an MFA in Writing for Children and Young Adults from Vermont College of Fine Arts. Born and raised in Vermont, she returned to her home state to raise her family and still lives between its green hills by a clear-running river.

cin salach has collaborated with musicians, painters, and, most recently, chefs and scientists for over thirty-five years. She feels called the loudest to hold space and create poetry experiences for people to speak their truths and remember love, even when they are most afraid, especially humans with dementia, and women with trauma.

Liz Garton Scanlon is the author of many beloved books for young people, including the Caldecott-honored picture book *All the World,* the *Bibsy Cross* chapter book series, and two middle grade novels. She writes with a monthly poetry collective, speaks and teaches across the country, and lives, votes and speaks up with all her heart in Austin, Texas.

Jim Schley is a book-discussion leader for Vermont Humanities, a contributing writer for the weekly newspaper *Seven Days*, and a freelance editor working mainly with the university presses at Wesleyan and Brandeis as well as New Directions. He lives on a land cooperative in Strafford, Vermont.

Retired humanities professor **Tom Schmidt** has placed more than seventy poems in journals and published two chapbooks and two collections, most recently *Rowing with Either Oar* (Solum Literary Press, 2024) and *Stranger in Parodies* (Kelsay Books, 2025). "Hotel Mar-a-Lago" was performed by Dana Lawrence at PoemCity in Montpelier on April 15, 2025.

Amabel Kylee Síorghlas lives in the hills of Vermont where she writes poetry, nonfiction, and fiction. Her cat Stella keeps her company. As a developmental editor, she helps others write books, especially memoir and fiction. She has an MFA in poetry from VCFA and an MA in fiction from UNH.

John Steffler's most recent books are *And Yet* (M&S, 2020) and *Forty-One Pages: On Poetry, Language and Wilderness* (URP, 2019). From 2006 to 2009 he was Parliamentary Poet Laureate of Canada. He lives in Eastern Ontario on unceded traditional Omamiwinini (Algonquin) territory.

Nancy Stewart has been a member of The Yogurt Poets in Concord, New Hampshire for almost thirty years. She has presented poetry-generating workshops at both the Massachusetts and New Hampshire Poetry Festivals. Her poems appear occasionally in journals and anthologies, including *Poet Showcase*, an anthology of New Hampshire poets.

Bianca Stone, currently Vermont's Poet Laureate, is the author of many books, including *What is Otherwise Infinite* (2022 Vermont Book Award) and *The Near and Distant World*, out from Tin House, January 2026. Her work has appeared in *The New Yorker, The Atlantic, Poets and Writers, The Nation* and the *Best American Poetry* series. In 2013 she co-founded the Ruth Stone House, where she organizes events, retreats, classes on poetry and poetic study, and hosts the *Ode & Psyche* Podcast.

Sarah B Sullivan (sarahbsullivan.com) of Northampton, Massachusetts, is a person, poet, teacher, physician, lesbian, ocean-lover, searcher. She is published here and there. Sarah served as chairperson for the Center for New Americans fundraiser, 30 Poems in November, for several years. She has been known to lead craft courses remotely and in person.

Joyce Thomas is the author of three poetry collections: *Some Things in This World* (Rootstock Publishing), *Washing Birds* (Main Street Rag), and *Skins* (Fithian Press). Professor Emerita at Vermont State University-Castleton, she has lived in Vermont since 1980.

Wyatt Townley is Poet Laureate of Kansas Emerita. Featured on NPR and in journals from *Newsweek* to *Paris Review, Yoga Journal* to *Scientific American*, her work hangs in the Space Telescope Science Institute, home of the Hubble. Her seventh book, *Making the Turn*, debuts with Lost Horse Press (fall 2026).

Lynn Ungar (lynnungar.com or substack.com/@lynnungar) is a writer, Unitarian Universalist minister and dog trainer who lives in Vancouver, Washington with her two Australian shepherds.

Henry Weinfield's most recent books of poems are *As the Crow Flies* (2021) and *An Alphabet* (2022), both published by Dos Madres Press. He is currently translating the poetry of Giacomo Leopardi and writing on Dante. He is Professor Emeritus of Liberal Studies at the University of Notre Dame.

Scott Withiam's third book of poetry, *Waste Management Facility*, was released by MadHat Press in July 2025. Withiam taught public school math and college English and writing, and also counseled for nonprofits. He is retired and now resides in Marblehead, Massachusetts, where he has quietly assumed his role of assuming good neighbors enjoy his daily practicing of drums.

Tim Wynne-Jones has written thirty-nine books including novels for adults, young adults and children, picture books, and four short story collections. He has won the Governor General's Award twice. His work has been published in ten languages in thirteen countries. In 2012, Tim was made an Officer of the Order of Canada.

Alyx Young is a twenty-two-year-old nonbinary queer poet currently living in Northern Vermont. Growing up in Southern New York with their parents and twin sister, Alyx was always an artsy kid and began writing poetry at around ten years old. This is Alyx's first published poem, and their dreams are only getting bigger!

Eva Zimet is a lifelong artist, coming of age in the theater and other arts and cultures. Her writing and illustrations appear in various journals, two books—*The Lost Grip* (poems) and *Lucy Dancer* (picture book, both by Rootstock Publishing)— and a screenplay lost in option-land.

Index of Contributors

Adams, Kauakanilehua Māhoe: "Today, I Figured I Should Finally Get Rid," 77
Ahlen, Pamela: "What We're Not Supposed to Say," 52
Allen, Amy: "Get Here," 61
Anderson, Doug: "Four Years," 193
Anlyan, Alexander: "Complicity," 21
Appelt, Kathi: "The Guadalupe Camp Mystic July 2025," 119
Bennett, Kelly: "Symphony in Hope Major," 203
Berry, Julie: "I have never loved America more," 113
Bergmann, Meredith: "The Ministry of Frost," 37; "Ask What," 51
Bird, James: "Rain or Shine," 38; "My Broken Mirror," 112
Blose, Pete: "Poets," 200
Bluestone, Stephen: "Aunt Esther," 30
Bourque, Jean-Blaise: "N'envoyez pas de fleurs" 206; "Do Not Send Flowers,"
        translation 210
Bryant, Louella: "Rising," 99
Cahill, S. J.: "The Pigeon Parade," 111; "Destination Despair," 157
Cheyne, Mary: "Contradiction," 108
daithí, daithí: "Wrecking Ball & the muskrats," 94
Darrow, Sharon: "Jon Batiste's Piano, Super Bowl 2025," 15;
        "What Am I Waiting For?," 53; "No Kings," 96
        "First Tipping Point, October 13, 2025," 167
        "The Survivors' Revolution," 197
deNiord, Chard: "Prophecy Against Those" 12; "In Thinking," 110;
        "Trump, a Philippic" 141
DePetrillo, Christine: "Candle," 27; "Dare," 195
Distler, Arlene Iris: "I woke up thinking of them," 24;
        "Passover Poem of Pain—Gaza," 60
Dominguez, Aria: "Subtext," 32
Dorantes, Raúl: "Corrido del ciclista," 67;
        "Corrido of the Cyclist" (*translated by Mary Hawley*), 69
        "Homenaje a los silbatos," 163;
        "Homage to the Whistles" (*translated by Mary Hawley,*) 165
Edmonds, Sandy: "Abject Cruelty," 63
Espada, Martín: "The Snake," 29; "The Iguanas Skitter Through the
        Cemetery by the Sea," 65
Faughnan, Cindy: "Don't Worry," 90
Foy, John: "Today's Horrorscope," 23; "Mary," 185
Franklin, Jennifer: "October 2025," 162
Fred, Elizabeth: "All That Life," 59; "Labor Day," 134
Galbraith, Robin: "White House Peace Vigil," 147
Ghebremichael, Simki: "¡SÍ, SE PUEDE!," 180
Giannino, Joanne: "On the way to the protest," 97
Gillis, Susan Gillis: "Cut Flowers," 212
González, Rigoberto: "Tanatofobia: Fear of Losing Your Mexican Mother," 64
Gorewitz, Shalom: "Raven's Protest Poem (from the film Unseen)," 122;
        "Have You Ever Met a Nefarian?" 161

Green, Chris Solís: "american dog," 142
Grimes, Nikki: "I Choke on Grace," 26
Gruber, Adrienne: "I Mostly Ignore the Horrors," 172
Hadas, Rachel: "Shouldering," 33; "The Truth as Well," 79;
    "Fire and Flood and Bureau Drawer," 103
    "Riding on a Cloud" 175
Harris, Amanda: "Poetic Justice," 201
Hauptman, Terry: "The Bataan Death March," 115;
    "Besiege Your Siege" 183
Hawes, Louise: "Baby Hitler," 35; "A Delicate Balance," 173
Hawley, Mary: "Corrido of the Cyclist," *translated* 69
    "Homage to the Whistles" *translated* 165
Hoover, Paul: "No Earth and No Heaven," 7; "Signs and Wonders," 45;
"As a Lion in Secret Places," 87; "The Dry Bones," 131
James, Susen: "What the Alt National Park Service Taught Me," 156
Janoo, Judith: "Neighbor," 17; "The Still Small Possibility," 62;
    "Take to the Streets, February 15, 2003," 95;
    "The Edge of the Gorge," 143; "Well Being," 199
Kanell, Beth: "Florida's Famous For:," 91
Katz, David: "The Green of Greenland," 19
Keizer, Garret: "You Think This is Hot?," 121
Knoll, Tricia: "I-89 from Vermont to Canada in Winter," 16
Kolber, Samantha: "It's the Beginning of the End and I'm Here to Tell You," 137
Koh, Jee Leong: "To the Tune of 'Veni redemptor gentium' by Ambrose of Milan," 73
Kramer, Nathalie Canessa: "I Long to See Her Unharmed
    Breathing Air the Earth Is Meant to Breathe," 177
Kunin, Madeleine May: "The Perfect Space," 105
Larios, Julie: "The Right Tyrant," 139
Lay-Sleeper, Ron: "That Gritty, Bright, Shadowless Sunlight," 76
Lea, Sydney: "Blues," 55
Levy, Hannah Eve: "The day a poet is murdered by ICE," 176
Lewis, Amanda West: "The Elephant in the Room," 154
Maguire, Gregory: "The Inheritance," 114
Majmudar, Amit: "Border Fugue," 28; "Rhapsody on a Line by Poe" 107
Mayo, Tim: "The Allegory of Elms," 205
McGhee, Alison: "Questionnaire," 71
Meriam, Mary: "Hunger," 72; "Forest," 169; "Mud Covenant," 170; "Colossus" 171
Minkin, Steve: "Shoelaces," 106
Moritz, Katie: "The climb," 153
Nichols-Frazer, "Erika: Believe Them," 14
Payne, J: "Stand by and Listen for the Whistle," 75
Pendergraft, Bill: "Mourning Dove," 213
Prentiss, Sean: "On the Day of the Election, I Think of the Video of M Nephew's
First Mountain Bike Ride with His Father, a Long Haul Covid Survivor," 9
Puican, Mike: "Americans in Love," 39; "Sunday Morning Haiku," 50;
    "Naming Light," 89; "The Candidates Debate," 135
Quimby, Katherine: "Palimpsest," 133
salach, cin: "A soul nosedives into a body doomed. "Angel bound.," 8;
    "How to Offer Hope," 123; "The World up Close," 204

Scanlon, Liz Garton: "All of Us, Singing," 214
Schley, Jim: "A Gathering," 206
Schmidt, Thomas: "Hotel Mar-a-lago," 40
Síorghlas, Amabel Kylee: "Fierce Compassion," 100
Steffler, John: "This Goes On and On," 117
Stewart, Nancy: "Jus Soli," 109
Stone, Bianca: "The Way Things Were Up Until Now," 48
Sullivan, Sarah B: "grace like time is everywhere," 182
Thomas, Joyce: "It disturbs me," 92
Townley, Wyatt: "Child at the Wheel," 34; "Election" 136;
        "The Country in the Mirror," 186
Ungar, Lynn: "Frog," 102
Weinfield, Henry: "Here pity only lives when it is dead," 56
Withiam, Scott: "Loss of Intrigue," 37; "Aftermath Posturing," 126; "Final Exam," 158
Wynne-Jones, Tim: "Pandemonium," 83;
        "I Am the Very Model of a Narcissistic Slanderer" 128
Young, Alyx: "The Watchlist," 145
Zimet, Eva: "Seed Shock," 31

Books by Sharon Darrow

Old Thunder and Miss Raney

The Painters of Lexieville

Through the Tempests Dark and Wild: A Story of Mary Shelley, Creator of Frankenstein

Trash

Yafi's Family: An Ethiopian Boy's Journey of Love, Loss, and Adoption (co-author, Linda Pettitt)

Worlds within Words: Writing and the Writing Life

now in a far sky: Vermont poems

Rainbow a Poem

We Grow Our Books in Montpelier, Vermont

Learn more about our titles in Fiction, Nonfiction, Poetry and Children's Literature at the QR code below or visit www.rootstockpublishing.com.